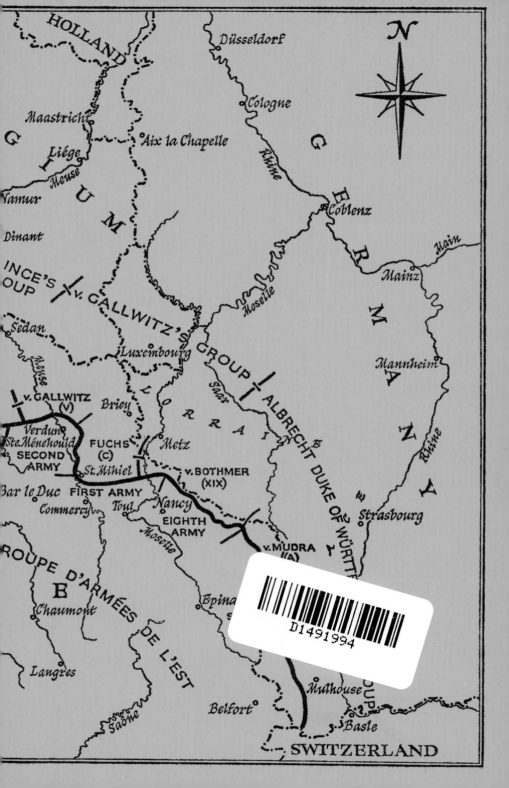

As From Kemmel Hill

ARTHUR BEHREND

As From Kemmel Hill

AN ADJUTANT
IN FRANCE AND FLANDERS,
1917 & 1918

LONDON
EYRE & SPOTTISWOODE

First published in 1963
© 1963 *by Arthur Behrend*
Printed in Great Britain by
C. Tinling & Co. Ltd.
Liverpool, London and Prescot
Catalogue No. 6/2495/1

In affectionate memory of

LIEUTENANT-COLONEL
ARTHUR HUGH THORP
C.M.G., D.S.O., R.G.A.

for two years my commander
in Flanders and in France

Acknowledgment

My thanks are due to Messrs George Newnes Ltd for permission to use part of a contribution which I made to *Twenty Years After*; also to the Imperial War Museum for the photographs facing pages 96 and 97.

Contents

Illustrations

Foreword

Kemmel Hill in Belgium, as many an old soldier of the 1914-18 war will remember, was one of the landmarks, even holdfasts, of the Western Front. Because of its superior height – it rose to a hundred and fifty feet – its wartime galleries commanded an extensive view of the Flanders plain and were used as an observation post by countless gunners, staff officers, sound-rangers, and the like. As a battery subaltern I observed from there myself several times in early 1917. From a brightly-coloured poster which I found, coveted, and stole from an empty and battered house in Kemmel village, it was clear that before the war Kemmel Hill with its densely-wooded slopes and Belle Vue inn and Belvedere tower had been a kind of amusement park for Belgian day trippers. In the bitter fighting of April 1918 it was suddenly overrun and captured by the Germans, but by the time that happened it had become an observation place of renown. Hence the title I have chosen.

This book, then, is my view of life in Flanders and France in 1917 and 1918, and in particular of our adventures during the great retreat of March 1918. By then I was Adjutant of a brigade of heavy artillery, and we happened to be in the line at the very junction point of Third and Fifth Armies. It is well known that Fifth Army was swamped and virtually disappeared as an organized force whereas Third Army bent but managed to hold. No criticism of the troops of Fifth Army is intended or implied; they were too thin on the ground, and in the initial assault the Germans were fortuitously helped by widespread mist, which in a number of places persisted throughout too much of the day. There was early-morning mist on our sector of the Third Army front too, but it soon dissipated.

[9]

The battle chapters could not have been written had it not been for the file of messages and signals received at our headquarters on March 21 and during the intensely exciting week which followed. The growing file went each night into the office tin box as brigade headquarters hastily packed up and again retreated, and there it was found a month later when I gave orders that the box must be tidied up and all its out-of-date contents destroyed. My Artillery Clerk, as the chief clerk of the brigade office was called, brought it to me as a minor curiosity, and because no one else wanted it and because of my hoarding instincts I put it in my bag and took it home next time I went on leave.

The battle story which I was thus able to reconstruct was printed by Heffers of Cambridge in 1921. Entitled *Nine Days*, it was then distributed and sold privately, mainly to officers and men of the brigade. A few copies were bought by the general public. The men for whom it was written had all been through the retreat themselves, and since they seemed to consider that the narrative reproduced the authentic atmosphere of the battle I have taken care not to alter the contemporary language in which I wrote my story forty years ago.

Perhaps I should here mention that the Germans were rarely if ever called Germans by the British army in the 1914-18 war. We sometimes called them 'Boches,' a descriptive word which the French had coined – it means 'square heads' – and when we really disliked them, which was not so very often, we called them 'Huns' – an equally descriptive word which I imagine sprang from the brain or pen of some unknown British propagandist at the time they swallowed Belgium. As often as not we called them 'Jerries,' but that was almost a term of endearment. Since I now find the repetitive use of 'Huns' and 'Boche' a trifle irritating, I have not over-used either of those words in this present narrative.

I realize, too, that army abbreviations, however familiar to some readers, may present difficulties to others. A glossary of those I have used will therefore be found at the end of the

Foreword, and in this way I have reduced the need for footnotes to a minimum.

.   .   .

To those young men of today who write about the 1914-18 war without having experienced it and who tear to shreds the reputation and professional conduct of its dead Generals, I should like to say that I think they tend to overlook the conditions of the time, the prevailing standards of military knowledge, and, most of all, the power and might of the German armies.

Though fortunately not present at the Battle of the Somme, I agree whole-heartedly with those who say, in retrospect, that it was a disaster – and for the Germans nearly as much as for ourselves. Passchendaele, as the Third Battle of Ypres is often called, I knew only too well, and I think now as I thought then; that the weather and therefore the water-logged earth was so consistently against us and for so long that it should have been called off weeks, even months, before it was. But the only qualification I have for saying so is the abiding memory of what my own eyes and feet told me.

Yet, whatever may be thought or written today about the tactical and strategic skill, or the lack of it, possessed by our higher command, we in France and Flanders in 1917 and 1918 had no complaints about the way in which we were administered. Our medical, transport, and supply services had advanced a long way since the days of the Boer and Crimean Wars. We were well fed and clothed; when we were wounded or sick we were admirably looked after; leave was given fairly, regularly, and generously; during my time with the B.E.F. there was no shortage of guns or ammunition, motors, maps, or indeed of anything. To us it seemed that the vast if at times cumbersome machine worked smoothly, and to us it was the last word in modernity. True the proper use of tanks was not yet understood, nor as yet was it clear to some of the high ups that the day of the horse as a battle-wagon was over. On the other hand aeroplanes, flimsy and slow though most of them were in those days, were competently managed and very bravely flown; to many it seemed a sad and hardly necessary change when the R.F.C. learned that in future it was to be known as the R.A.F.

Surprising though it may seem to those writers I have mentioned, it was not our habit to criticize our top Generals. A few soldier-writers did, I know, but they soon got their tails twisted for their trouble. For we did not know our Generals, nor did they seem to want us to know them. I saw Haig but once, and then only from a distance. Whatever the capacity of his brain, he was a fine and upright figure on a horse; he looked the part and thus left one in no doubt that he was the sort of man well able to shoulder his responsibilities.[1]

It was noticeable and therefore common knowledge that Second Army under Plumer cared for and looked after its troops better than any of our other Armies. Hence Plumer, a small white-haired man with pink cheeks, was rated as a good General, and his Battle of Messines – for he, or maybe Harrington his Chief of Staff, planned and executed it – was so much a model of what a battle for limited objectives should be that it was almost a pleasure to take part in it. Not that I ever saw him, and it is perhaps through a photograph that he remains in my mind's eye as a father, even grandfather, figure. Only the other day a friend, glancing through what I have written, mentioned that he had attended some course at Second Army headquarters, and at the end Plumer addressed them and said, "When I send a staff officer up the line and he comes back and tells me what he found wrong, I stop him and say, 'I want to know what you found right'."

Nor did I see the tougher and more masculine Byng, yet we served in his Third Army for more than a year. Though, to be fair to him, while he was out one day inspecting reserve-line defences he paid one of our batteries a chance and un-

---

[1] It shocked me, many years later, to learn of his pettiness, obstinacy, and obtuseness; surely he was the first British military leader to hang himself by his own diaries and letters. See *Private Papers of Douglas Haig*, edited Robert Blake: London, 1952.

announced visit and created a good impression by his manner and because he talked pleasantly to a gun team and asked its limber-gunner a number of sensible questions. He also inspected the brigade at the end of July 1918 – 48 officers and 756 other ranks, I see – but I was on leave. To quote his staff officer's follow-up letter, "The Army Commander addressed the brigade and battery commanders and warmly appreciated the good work done by batteries and Motor Transport personnel during the operations from 21st March to 6th April. He commented on various points such as the state of small arms ammunition carried in bandoliers, also a few rifle bolts which should have been cleaner and required attention. He suggested that A.S.C. personnel should be given opportunities for rifle practice, and that some arrangements should be made for keeping down the plague of flies in the cookhouses. He desired that in future when a Heavy Brigade parades for inspection the men should appear in Marching Order, also that all men who carry rifles must always carry small arms ammunition." Nevertheless the report concludes, "The brigade presented a fine appearance on parade and the turn-out with the exceptions above noted was very satisfactory."

It was clear that Byng had not been a gunner.

Gough was only a name to us, but whatever his grievances – he later claimed, and with ultimate success, that he had been given inadequate resources for his task – most of us thought it fair that he got his bowler hat because of the collapse of Fifth Army.

The only Generals I knew personally and actually spoke to were mere Brigadier- or Major-Generals, and not many of those. The one we thought best was Russell, commander of the magnificent New Zealand Division. As may be read later in this book, my only interview with Harper, dour commander of the equally redoubtable 51st Highland Division, was anything but a social occasion. The M.G.R.A. (Major-General Royal Artillery) of IV Corps, or perhaps of Third Army, who came to see us once or twice and whose name I forget, looked a bit of an ass – and my Colonel, who knew him, said he was one. When talking to our batteries he was apt to rub his hands together and say in genial tones, "Splendid, splendid!" For that reason – but I myself cannot think why – the nickname he earned was Pork Butcher. But he was kindly, and at least he was a gunner. It was our Corps Commander who, paying a visit to our 9·2 battery and seeing the words INSPECTED AT GIB painted on the sides of their howitzers, said in surprise, "I'd no idea these guns had been to Gibraltar." None of the officers, not even the battery commander, wished to tell him that the letters GIB stood for General Inspection Branch.

Glossary of Army Terms
and Abbreviations

AAA	In Signals practice of the time signified full stop.
Ack	The letter A in the Signals language of the time.
A.P.M.	Assistant Provost-Marshal, staff officer of military police.
B.C.	Battery Commander.
B.C. Post	Battery Commander's Post, the command post of battery.
Bdr.	Bombardier, the Royal Artillery equivalent of corporal.
Beer	The letter B in the Signals language of the time.
B.E.F.	British Expeditionary Force. Applied to our armies in France and Belgium, but not elsewhere.
B.Q.M.S.	Battery Quartermaster-Sergeant.
Cat	Caterpillar tractor, a tracked vehicle used for towing heavier guns such as the 9·2 howitzer.
C.C.S.	Casualty Clearing Station.
Corps Heavies	Familiar term for Corps Heavy Artillery Headquarters, the formation responsible to a Corps Commander for all the heavy artillery in a Corps.
C.R.A.	Commander, Royal Artillery. Usually the senior artillery staff officer of a Division.
C.R.E.	Commander, Royal Engineers. Usually the senior engineer staff officer of a Division.

dis	disconnected. Thus, in the case of a telephone line, broken or out of action.
Don	The letter D in the Signals language of the time.
D.R., also Don R.	Dispatch-rider.
E.F.C.	Expeditionary Force Canteen, the 1914-18 equivalent of N.A.A.F.I.
Elephant	Type of sectional steel shelter with curved top, forerunner of the Anderson air raid shelter.
F.O.O.	Forward Observation Officer. Any battery officer sent forward to observe from an O.P.
F.W.D.	Four-Wheel Drive, as its name implies more adaptable and powerful than the usual lorry and therefore used for towing 6-inch howitzers.
Garrison Gunner	Any member of the Royal Garrison Artillery.
G.O.C.	General Officer Commanding. Usually of Corps Commander status.
G.S.O.1	General Staff Officer, 1st grade.
G.S. wagon	General Service wagon, the horse-drawn cart in general use by the British army during 1914-18 war.
H.E.	High Explosive.
How.	Usual abbreviation for Howitzer. See footnotes on pages 37 and 70 for fuller explanation.
H.V. or H.Vic	High Velocity. Particularly of a shell fired from a high-velocity gun (which a howitzer was not).
M.P.	Military Policeman.
Nissen hut	Type of large and easily-erected hut with wooden ends and sides and roof of curved steel, first used in 1914-18 war.
O.C.	Officer Commanding. Any officer in actual command of a battery or in-

	fantry company or platoon etc. Not to be confused with C.O. (Commanding Officer), the proper description of a Lieutenant-Colonel in command of an artillery brigade or an infantry battalion.
O.P.	Observation Post.
Piece	Slightly archaic term for heavy gun or howitzer. Or, in some cases, for a portion thereof.
R.A.	Royal Artillery.
Red Cap	Military policeman, so called because of the colour of his cap.
R.G.A.	Royal Garrison Artillery. Branch of Royal Artillery; its early role was to man coast defences, hence its name. In the 1914-18 war the R.G.A. produced the officers and men required for several hundred Siege (or Heavy) Batteries. No longer exists as a separate entity, having been merged into the much larger Royal Artillery.
R.S.M.	Regimental Sergeant-Major.
S.A.A. cart	Horse- or mule-drawn cart for carrying Small Arms Ammunition, i.e. rifle ammunition.
Sapper	Any member of the Royal Engineers.
Siege Park	Central depot, usually on Corps basis, where Army Service Corps lorries would be found parked.
S.O.S.	As at sea the signal for help. Often initiated by front line infantry by means of rocket signals.
S.O.S. Lines	The line or bearing (and elevation) upon which guns were laid on pre-arranged targets, usually by night, to enable them to respond to S.O.S. call without delay.

B

Toc 1, Toc 2, etc.   Our private code-names for the batteries of the Brigade. See footnote on page 43 for explanation.

Yellow Cross   Type of German mustard gas.

As From Kemmel Hill

CHAPTER I

England, 1916

One still evening during the summer of 1916 I heard the guns of France for the first time. I was alone. The blue sky was unclouded and there was no wind; before me the sea was gently washing the shingle of Cooden Beach. So valueless – in those days – was the virgin heathland upon which I stood that the War Office had been able to desecrate it with the hutted camp to which twenty minutes earlier I had delivered a draft of gunner reinforcements, decent steady men who had given no trouble during the stops and changes of the slow journey by South Eastern & Chatham Railway from Sheerness. The noise to which I listened came from far away across the Channel and was not to be confused with distant thunder. It was unmistakably gunfire, many times more lavish than anything I had heard in Gallipoli, a continuous rumble unchanging in tone and so steady in volume that the rabbits went on playing and feeding beside me undisturbed. Although I did not know it, the orchestra of guns had reached the crescendo of the overture to the Battle of the Somme.

.   .   .

Let me explain how I, an infantry subaltern in my previous book,[1] came to be delivering a draft of gunners.

My sick leave of two months had been extended to four, and since a further medical board had then decreed six months of Light Duty and added the injunction that I was not to go east again, I now had no hope of rejoining my own battalion. I was waiting at home for posting orders when the Army Council published an Instruction which drew attention to the shortage of artillery officers likely to arise by

[1] *Make Me A Soldier: A Platoon Commander in Gallipoli* (1961).

reason of the proposed expansion of the Royal Regiment of Artillery and went on to say that applications for transfer would be welcomed from junior officers of other arms.

I put in my application through the proper channels, and the reason I applied was not because I disliked the infantry. But I did dislike, and very strongly, the prospect of six months of light duty in Blackpool, where my depot battalion was stationed. Furthermore, so I had been told, it had many more junior officers on its strength than it knew what to do with.

My transfer came through so quickly that the need envisaged by the Army Council must have been acute. So there was I, a Gallipoli veteran in other people's eyes if not my own, wearing the badges and buttons of a branch of the service about which I knew absolutely nothing.

I was posted to the headquarters of the Lancashire & Cheshire R.G.A. at Crosby, and quickly joined a young officers' course in elementary gunnery. Our instructor was the Adjutant, Mackenzie by name, a tall ex-ranker with a pointed waxed moustache, and from him I learned the simpler mysteries of ballistics, range tables, and initial corrections. I do not remember what else I learned, but I do remember an invitation from the R.S.M. to witness a contest which took place one night in the sergeants' mess. Within its ranks the Lancashire & Cheshire had one or two champion beer drinkers, and our best man had challenged the adjacent depot of the South Wales Borderers. I cannot recall the winner. Our man put down fourteen pints – or was it sixteen? – in as many minutes and then passed out, and I have not yet forgotten the noise, the excitement, the beer-laden and smoky atmosphere, and the smell of several hundred closely-crowded men. Perhaps that is why I have long been allergic to beer.

From headquarters I was posted to Seaforth, a small and ancient fort overlooking the narrows of the Mersey and thus constituting the northern half of its inner defences – which I am certain were never tested by the Germans. By now my period of light duty was nearly over, and from Seaforth I was sent to a larger and more salubrious fort at Sheerness. Its name was Garrison Point, or GP for short. I was glad to leave Seaforth because I did not care for my battery commander. A month later he was posted to GP too, and that at the time seemed awkward because he took an early opportunity of telling me he knew quite well I had hoped to escape him. After that our relations became much easier. He taught me to eat – and enjoy – oysters, and since I had a motorcycle I was sometimes sent to Whitstable to buy them for the battery mess. The oyster trade of 1916 was in the doldrums, and you could get a keg of fifty, dripping from the sea, for ten bob.

When granted overnight leave we could tear off to London to see Violet Loraine in the *Bing Boys* or Oscar Asche in *Chu Chin Chow*; I suppose there were speed limits in those days too but there was no one to enforce them, and the early morning emptiness of the Old Kent Road is a memory I shall not forget. Petrol of course was severely rationed, and to make it go further we broke the law by mixing it with paraffin; I still remember the consternation on a brother subaltern's face when, ready for off, he kick-started his machine and saw the resulting explosion blow the sparking-plug from its seat and send it flying skywards through two thicknesses of petrol tank.

There were military duties too. We performed gun drill by the hour. We dressed up the men in highly-polished leather bandoliers and took them for brisk keep-fit route marches. Every so often we fired our 6-inch guns at towed targets, and sometimes we had a day's sail in the towing craft, plotting the fall of rounds and chivying out of range the Thames barges which usually disregarded our signals and our antics. On one occasion Garrison Orders detailed me as attending officer to a regular captain under close arrest and awaiting court martial on some forgotten charge; for some equally forgotten reason his court martial was delayed and we had to live in each other's exclusive company for a fortnight. Poor devil, I got to know him and like him. In short I found life and discipline in the gunners very different from that in my old battalion; the shadow of death seemed much further away, and, or so it appeared, no one here bothered about what might be said or thought of him in his home town after the war was over.

Sheerness in those days was a naval base of enough importance to be guarded by a whole nest of forts of varying shapes and sizes, and within the Naval Dockyard there was a large and old-established R.A. Mess redolent with peace-time inhibitions. Seeing that it was now being kept alive on enforced subscriptions from Territorials and other temporary oddities, we found it hard, even to the point of saying so, that though the Mess Committee took our money they would not let us drink our share of their stocks of vintage port.

But Sheerness could produce greater excitements than that. On the morning of May 31 the Third Battle Squadron steamed out in line ahead through the hastily-opened boom. *Dreadnought* was leading, followed by *King Edward VII* and the other older battleships of that class. I happened to be in the fire-control room of GP at the time and saw it all, a thrilling sight to one who only a few years before had been a schoolboy member of the Navy League. They were on their way to the Battle of Jutland. A day or two later they returned, and in exactly the same formation. Their speed was so slow, or the distance so great, that the battle was over before they reached it. The Fountain, a public house just outside the dockyard gates, did big trade that night.

For a few delightful weeks during the early autumn I was sent off to take charge of four venerable 15-pounder field guns cunningly hidden from public view in open-ended barns and imitation haystacks on the low cliffs of Sheppey. They covered a stretch of coast where, just before the war, Blue Fleet under Jellicoe had outwitted Red Fleet by landing an invading force of marines and soldiers. Also under my command I had a realistic but bogus 6-inch gun; it was fashioned from a tree trunk. I came in for a General's inspection there too, but it passed off well. The General could not take his eyes off the mushrooms which grew more thickly than the daisies on the neglected lawn of my villa billet, over every field round the guns as well. Yes, we had all been living on them for days, I told him, and the moment the inspection ended he asked for empty boxes and sent his A.D.C. to fill them. He departed saying it was a good show, but whether he was referring to guns or mushrooms I do not know.

Such was the England of 1916 as I remember it, a picture brightened by a primitive yet effective form of cheerful propaganda and not yet darkened by the lengthening casualty lists of the Battle of the Somme. Business as Usual was still the motto, for in no other way – so it was generally thought – could the war be won more easily or more quickly. I was becoming restless because this was not my idea of soldiering, and I do not say that smugly. Relief was at hand, and as a first step I was sent to Horsham for a course on Siege Artillery.

CHAPTER II

Siege Battery

In the later autumn I was posted to 279 Siege Battery. When I arrived I found a battery in nothing but name, but it formed and grew up quickly. Half its officers and men came from my own unit, the Lancashire & Cheshire R.G.A., the other half from the true north of England and from Scotland. My battery commander was too young and inexperienced for command, but he was agreeable and considerate, he did not throw his quite substantial weight about, and he was personally courageous. He was very fortunate in his second-in-command, a solicitor from Lancashire who had been one of my companions at Seaforth. I shall call him Tom because that was his nickname; for some equally ridiculous reason my battery commander insisted on calling me Charles.

Tom was one of those men who sticks to things; he remained with the battery throughout most of the war but shamefully was not promoted to command it when the battery commander was wounded. After the war he joined Cadbury's on the firm's legal side: there his qualities were recognized and appreciated, and before he retired he became one of their directors. Of the subalterns I remember best an unconscious comic of good value named Baskett, who was killed, and Money – known as Chiozza, his real name in this case – a merry young bank clerk who emigrated to Australia soon after the war. He came to see me recently, his first visit to England for forty years. By guts and pioneering he had made good, but in the process he had become more Australian than any Australian. He had come over to see what the old country was like, even to buy a place to retire to, but found things so little to his liking that after a fortnight he booked his passage back to Sydney. "No, Charles, you won't see me here again," he said. "You're still a bloody stuffy lot, and the trouble with you all is that you don't yet know it."

But I am beating the band as the saying is; I have spoken of these old-time friends mainly to show that we became a united, happy, and I think contented battery. We mobilized at Devizes during the January snows, and there we received our new 6-inch howitzers. As was the custom we painted a name on each barrel; my section voted to call our two CHARLIE CHAPLIN and GEORGE FORMBY respectively. After a brief visit to Tintown at Lydd to conduct full-charge shoots on the ranges in order to test our guns and ourselves and to satisfy the resident instructors of gunnery, we embarked for France.

As *Mona's Queen* sidled into Havre through brown opaque water and tied up gently against the stone quay, I could not help thinking that this was a very different landing from my previous one at Cape Helles.[1] There, below the pontoon we had to cross from *River Clyde*, the water was six feet deep and so crystal clear that on the bottom we could see, lying in perfect preservation, the uniformed bodies of the soldiers who had been hit or who had fallen in while scrambling ashore ten days earlier.[2]

From tranquil but busy Havre we staged north to Bailleul, then into Flanders, and a few days later my section was firing at Germans from a copse of spidery trees alongside the road on the northern outskirts of Kemmel.

No battery could have been given an easier introduction to war. In the Kemmel of early 1917 there seemed little need for deep dug-outs. Indeed none existed, perhaps because it had long since been known that in Flanders, winter and summer alike, the shallowest hole filled with water almost while it was being dug. If protection was required – and it struck me that protection was not in fashion – there was no alternative but to put up a breastwork built of sandbags, and what

[1] *Make Me A Soldier*, p. 66.
[2] Probably 1st Bn. Royal Munster Fusiliers. With their packs and their three days' iron rations and their 200 rounds of ammunition a man they did not come up again, and there they still lay.

British soldier has ever been willing to earn his pay by filling sandbags? At first, therefore, the battery lived, ate, and slept above ground, and it was not till a month or two later when the shells really began to fall that men's thoughts turned to shacks with roofs of corrugated iron which some covered with a few inches of earth. Such security was imagined and not real.

There was always genuine devastation and destruction to be seen in Ypres a few miles to our north, and I for one went to see it. But in villages like Kemmel the houses were still fit to be used as billets, at any rate on their ground floors, and trees still stood upright in Ploegsteert Wood. From an observation post on its fringe I saw my first live Germans, two soft-capped grey shapes stealing, then scuttling, through the undergrowth. Poor Plugstreet Wood was finally flattened by both sides during the preliminary bombardment and counter-bombardment of the Battle of Messines.

On June 17 at zero hour – 3.10 AM – the nineteen great mines on Messines Ridge exploded just as monster mines should, but to my disappointment it was too dark to see the resulting turmoil. Similarly the noise in our gun-pits was already so loud that we heard nothing extra. During the first afternoon of the battle there was a perceptible lull. Messines Ridge was now ours, and in fulfilment of a vow I walked off, crossed both the old front lines, and returned with a cigarette tin filled with red dust from the rubble of the brick-stack which had once been the high chimney of Wytschaete Hospice or Workhouse. Throughout the previous months our guns had registered on it twice daily.

I should like to put on record one further memory of the Battle of Messines. However little it interested me then, it fascinates me today that during this battle, and for weeks before, the 16th Irish Division and the 36th Ulster Division lived and fought side by side, got on with each other splendidly, admired each other, supported each other, and at times even pulled each other's chestnuts out of the fire. . . .

When the battle ended we moved to Ypres, under orders to place our guns on the blasted road which ran beside the wide but stagnant moat. It was an indecently exposed gun position, but artillery of every calibre was now massing and many batteries were worse off. Our casualties began to mount, and here Bombardier Fulton, not without risk to himself, achieved the battery's first Military Medal. However we soon got used to living uncertainly, and for me it did not last long because a couple of weeks later I left the battery in a most unexpected manner.

We were now in a new Brigade, or Group as they were then still called, of Heavy Artillery, and our new Colonel, a regular, was a wizened little man with greying hair, round steel-rimmed spectacles, and bandy legs. He came to see us at frequent intervals and without prior warning, and though he did not say much he clearly knew his mind. Moreover he expected any order he gave to be obeyed instantly and without one word of argument. Our previous Colonel had been easy-going and rarely seen; this new one had already put the wind up John our battery commander.

One evening when I came into the mess shack for supper John peered at me and said, "The Colonel's fed up with his present Adjutant and wants a new one, and he asked me if I've anyone I can recommend. The man terrifies me, but I've recommended you, Charles."

"Why?" I asked, not all that pleased.

"Because it's time you got promotion and there's none for you here."

"Is his present Adjutant coming here to take over my section?"

"Not damned likely," my battery commander replied. "I've said I won't have him. Pack up here and report to Group at one o'clock tomorrow if you want the job. It's up to you now."

The Group occupied an undamaged farmhouse at Vlamertinghe midway between Poperinghe and Ypres, and as I arrived in the battery car I saw a middle-aged man sunning himself against the front door. He was a captain, I noticed.

"Who are you?" was his greeting. He was wearing the badges of the R.A.M.C.

"I've been told to report here as Adjutant."

"Huh," he sneered, and he looked me up and down for a few moments. "You're the third we've had in two months. *You* won't last long."

CHAPTER III

Colonel Thorp

Colonel Thorp was not a man who inspired affection nor could he ever be accused of seeking it, but whether you liked him or not – and in all honesty not many did – everyone respected him. In my own case the better I got to know him the more I became attached to him, but it was a slow process not without set-backs.

During my first months at brigade headquarters he no doubt looked upon me as ignorant and untrained. But from the start he trusted me, and since I never felt afraid of him the relationship soon established between us worked surprisingly well, although his idiosyncrasies were well-nigh unbelievable. He was self-disciplined and without fear, he hardly ever relaxed, and he had the highest possible sense of duty. He saw through eye-wash instantly, he hated unnecessary verbiage – for which his word was 'quack' – and heaven help the unwitting officer, N.C.O., or gunner who forgot or had not been told that there were only three permissible answers to his questions – "Yes", "No", or "I don't know". Yet, as I often had to explain to newcomers and to others who did not know him, he was by no means the ogre he might seem.

Physically he was a poor specimen, and without his spectacles he was lost; therefore he was not interested in sport or athletics, and I suspect for that reason, though he never talked about his younger days, he had had a thin time at school and perhaps at Woolwich too. Technically he was a first-class Garrison Gunner, and from what he said on occasions during rare moments of semi-relaxation it was clear he had reached the first peak of his life's ambition when sent to France in 1915 in command of the battery which consisted of the B.E.F.'s one and only 9·2 gun on a railway mounting. Sometimes, too, he spoke nostalgically of life in sunny Jamaica, his army station for a number of years. Notwithstanding his physical defects he was tireless, and hard though he drove others he drove himself harder.

On the debit side he practically never praised, his temper could be short, he resented any form of criticism because he believed he was always right, as indeed he usually was. This resentment of criticism was the cause of the only major row I had with him, and I shall tell that story later. He disliked higher authority on principle; in consequence higher authority did not like him. He was often sarcastic, his reading was restricted to orders and intelligence summaries – and he forgot nothing. His sole hobby was Salvage, about which he was fanatical. He had no friends I knew of, either within the Royal Regiment or outside; those gunner Generals who sometimes came round from Corps or Army, men who were surely his contemporaries, greeted him formally and treated him with reserve. He wrote four letters a year, and in reply received two letters and two parcels; the letters came from Miss Emma Thorp, presumably his sister, at some rectory in Norfolk, the parcels from Abbott's Phiteezi Boots in London. Each contained one new pair of trench boots.

He was not interested in food; he drank a very little gin or whisky, and only after sundown. We thought him a bachelor for life; he let us down by marrying after the war. He objected to padres whatever their denomination, and had so little use for them that he successfully resisted several attempts to plant one on us as a kind of paying guest; indeed the chaplains' hierarchy must have had a special file about him, because in the end secular pressure was sought and applied, and he had to submit. But it was only half a victory for the church – the man who arrived, a harmless if unwarlike type, was at once dispatched to live with a battery. It was a strange kink in one who, so we gathered, had himself been a parson's son.

He was a tiger about orders. Being over-ready to condemn

the form, even sometimes the substance, of those we received
from above, he was over-particular about his own. He wrote
many of them himself in long-hand, always in clear and
delightful writing, and with never a loose phrase. 'You will
do such and such a thing . . .'' was equivocal to his way of
thinking; he therefore allowed the recipient no latitude and
left him in no doubt by stating, 'You are to . . .' There was
hell to pay if any acknowledgement which he had demanded
was not forthcoming or had not been dispatched quickly
enough; a new battery might be forgiven a first or second
lapse, but thereafter the presence of the battery commander
would be required to explain in person. It was equally widely
known that he was a stickler about telephone drill, that his
temperature rose to flash-point if asked to 'hold the line a
moment' because someone wished to speak to him, and that
even under otherwise stable conditions use of the word
'Hullo?' caused detonation.

There was yet another trap for the unwary telephonist.
On occasions of urgency he was prone to ring up a battery
and say "Colonel Thorp speaking. Is an officer handy?"
By 'handy' – and all telephonists were expected to know
this – he meant was there an officer beside the phone or
sufficiently close to it to come within a few seconds. Every
telephonist was expected to know, too, that any answer
other than "Yes, sir," or "No, sir," was pure quack. The
Colonel's telephone voice was not conversational, and if the
reply was "Yes, sir," he would say gruffly, "Put him on."
Contrary to popular fears there was no irritation if the
answer was "No, sir," and according to circumstances he
would reply, "I shall hold on while you send for him," or
"Send for him quickly and tell him to call me back."

As an inventor of succinct and often apt code words – for
the purpose of shortening signals, reducing quack generally,
and perhaps of mystifying the enemy – he was in his element,
and if a particularly good one was evolved he might be heard
to chuckle aloud. A gun out of action had to be reported to
us by the battery concerned as KITCHENER; when once more
in action it became DERBY (after the then War Minister). He

C

delighted, too, in code words – of his own production, not of mine or of anyone else's – for prearranged shoots, and of these BUMP and WHIPPET are nice examples. For a period he showed such marked preference for girls' names, always those with the more old-fashioned ring like CLARICE, DOLLY, GERTIE, FANNY, PANSY, LILLY, NELL, even LIZZY and TINA, that I used to wonder if they reminded him – to quote one of his favoured clichés – of his misspent youth. Did YVONNE recall –another of his clichés – some dim and distant week-end in Paris? Any shoot in support of the infantry was prefixed COMRADE, whereupon the batteries could be relied upon to do more than their damnedest. One Sunday morning Corps Heavies ordered the whole brigade to engage four different targets in quick succession, and while pin-points were being checked and our own orders prepared I well remember the chuckles which accompanied MATTHEW, MARK, LUKE, and JOHN out of the Colonel's hat.[1]

Because he considered it a soldier's duty to be brave at all times he despised honours and awards, even immediate ones, and I had standing instructions to send in a Nil return whenever Corps Heavies asked us for half-yearly recommendations. He also despised Leave, which he thought unnecessary because it interfered with winning the war, and a classic comedy occurred when Corps compelled him to take one himself – his only leave in two years. During his absence the brigade was commanded by Major Pargiter – forgetful about names, the Colonel was always liable to call him Partiger – the senior battery commander, one of our few regulars and an outstanding soldier. In the middle of it a signal came in from Corps Heavies asking us to submit the name of a Warrant Officer or senior N.C.O. for what was described in the message as 'a French military medal'. I showed it to Pargiter, and commented that in accordance with the Colonel's wishes the reply must be Nil.

"Certainly not," Pargiter replied. "I'm commanding this brigade now. Whom shall we recommend?"

[1] Also the names of four notorious copses in enemy-held territory just west of Serre.

"Well, what about the R.S.M.? As you know he's an old woman, but he's a decent chap and he's done God knows how many years in the army. And it's only a French thing."

"Right." Pargiter too was a man of few words. "Send his name in."

I did, and thought no more about it till the Colonel returned and looked through the files. "What's this?" he demanded.

"Major Pargiter ordered me to send it in, sir," I replied smugly.

The Colonel grunted; it was clear he did not like it.

He liked it still less when six weeks later Corps Heavies told us a French General would arrive at our headquarters at noon the following day to present R.S.M. Oatley with his medal, and that the personnel of brigade headquarters would turn out in review order to do him the honours. The Colonel was speechless, but there was nothing he could do to stop it.

The General arrived, accompanied by several French staff officers. The medal turned out to be the Médaille Militaire, the highest honour the French could confer on any soldier – so high that it carried with it a pension of I think a hundred francs a year for life. The General pinned the medal on R.S.M. Oatley's breast and kissed him; then he turned and kissed Colonel Thorp too.

I must say the Colonel took it better than expected, because in some way it must have appealed to his primitive sense of humour. It certainly appealed to ours.

Among the other officers at brigade headquarters there was Captain Vincent R.A.M.C., whom I have already mentioned. He was elderly – a good forty-five and therefore much the same age as the Colonel – and he told us that before the war he had been a Harley Street children's specialist. The batteries did not welcome him and said he drank, but I do not know about that. In my memory he was an uncomfortable man, and he seemed to think the worst of everyone. He did not much care for going out and about, but sometimes he joined the Colonel on his daily rounds. I see them now sitting side by side in the back of the open Vauxhall; the spread of the tin hat each was wearing allowed of no intimate conversation. Not that they would have spoken much anyhow, because neither liked the other. In our small mess he was sardonic, and as soon as each meal was over he retired to his own quarters. The only company he did not seem to mind was that of Bdr. White his medical orderly, a tall and gentle gunner whom the men liked because he did his work quietly and well, and I often saw them trudging off together with the medical box slung over the orderly's shoulder. I am sorry to write so hardly of a fellow-soldier; in retrospect I feel sorry for him because he was friendless and because with us he was a complete misfit.

On the other hand our Signals officer was delightful. He was a year younger than me, his name was Gardiner. In 1914 he had won an open scholarship to Pembroke College, Cambridge, and in after years he became a civil engineer of distinction. He was fearless at his job, and – when necessary – not afraid of standing up to the Colonel. His signal section was partly composed of men who had been Post Office linesmen, and because of his leadership it was equally fearless and always on the top line. His only faults in those days were illegible handwriting, a habitual tendency to oversleep, and a certain untidiness in dress. When talking about books one day he told me how his father, a housemaster at Epsom College, had befriended a young and unknown assistant master who had recently joined the staff, and on one occasion had even asked him to dinner. Hugh Walpole repaid the debt by putting a cruelly distorted account of the evening and of his host, his host's wife too, into the pages of *Mr Perrin and Mr Traill*.

CHAPTER IV

Third Battle of Ypres

The main role of heavy artillery during that summer of 1917 was counter-battery work, that is to say the neutralizing and slow destruction of the opposing heavy artillery, and it was in this invisible and unending duel between giants that the batteries of our Group were largely engaged during my first weeks as its Adjutant. Yet 'invisible' is not entirely correct, because it was always fascinating to study and compare the 'before' and 'after' air photographs faithfully taken and distributed by our co-operation squadron of the Royal Flying Corps, and I was often astonished by the recovery powers of many an enemy battery which should have been, and indeed apparently was, obliterated by the photographically-spectacular effects of a concentrated shoot.

For that kind of shoot rarely meant less than a hundred rounds per gun from a battery which consisted of six 6-inch or 8-inch guns.[1] But every gunner knows that the shell which scores a direct hit on a gun or its detachment is as rare as the golf ball which finds its hole in one, and all too often the battery which had been our target was quickly on its feet again, firing away as actively as before. Seemingly all we had done was to silence it for a few hours, and, if a battery which had been engaged once or twice before, to increase the

---

[1] Our guns were all howitzers, a howitzer being the type of gun which fires a shell at a high elevation with a comparatively low muzzle-velocity – indeed so low that as often as not if you stood behind a howitzer and looked up at the moment of firing you could catch a glimpse of the shell during the fraction of a second when it reached the top of its trajectory; it looked exactly like a squarely-hit golf ball. Because of its lower muzzle-velocity the howitzer has a shorter range than that of a high-velocity gun. But for the same reason it has a longer life, the 'wear' on the barrel being less.

already fantastic number of shell craters surrounding its position.[1]

This game could be played in reverse. The first thing to do, if your own battery happened to be at the receiving end, was to get into action again, and as soon as possible. Indeed a battery carrying out a set task was expected to keep on firing, even if under fire itself. Thus a triangular drama could, and often did, develop if British battery A, while conducting a shoot on German battery B, was engaged out of the blue by German battery C. Provided battery C could be located quickly enough by means of sound-rangers or by an observer in a kite-balloon or aeroplane or from a ground observation post, the counter-battery department of Corps Heavies usually had either a battery up its sleeve or one which could be switched from some less pressing task to join in the party.

All this artillery activity was of course taking place in preparation for the Third Battle of Ypres, and on its opening day, July 31, our orderly officer, an Irishman named Linden, was killed in the Group observation post on Freezenberg Ridge. His companion Strain, an able and charming young officer from one of the batteries, was killed at his side. The Colonel had detailed and briefed them himself, and when the news of their deaths reached us he almost broke down.

The same evening we moved forward from our farmhouse at Vlamertinghe into a gallery of mined dug-outs deep inside the eastern ramparts of Ypres. Their entrance adjoined the Menin Gate, the Ypres equivalent of London's Marble Arch. When Captain Vincent saw our new headquarters he poured out a stiff whisky and pronounced them unfit for human habitation, and though we occupied them for two months I am sure he was right. We worked by artificial light, lived and ate by it too, and the air was always stale and sometimes foul. But because of the thickness of the ramparts we thought we were fairly safe – an illusion, since in a similar gallery alongside ours half the personnel of another Heavy Artillery Group was soon to be trapped and set alight.

[1] See plate facing page 81.

Our batteries had moved forward too; they were now firing from the mud on either side of the Potijze Road, and within a mile of our headquarters. Owing to the shape and flatness of the Salient they were visible to thousands of German eyes, and only the number of batteries in the same plight saved each individual one from total destruction. Because of the mud and the shell craters and the constant shelling it was always difficult to keep them supplied with ammunition; for the same reasons it was equally difficult for them to take care of it once they got it. Indeed the mud was nearly as formidable an enemy as the Germans.

It was the Colonel's custom to go round the batteries at least once daily, and Gardiner and I took it in turns to go with him. But now that both sides were firmly locked in battle – on our sector after a minute initial advance the situation was stalemate – it became increasingly suicidal to walk about in front of Ypres in daylight, and even the Colonel was forced to change his habits. Like everyone else engaged in the battle the German gunners needed sleep, and experience showed that usually, but not always, they knocked off from dawn till breakfast-time. These few comparatively quiet hours became our opportunity for visiting.

My memories of those grim expeditions are confused, because all seemed so alike. We went on foot, our gas masks slung at the ready. I cannot remember that we used them, but the garlic stench of mustard gas, hangover of the nightly area strafes, still haunts me. Each day we saw the same sorry sights – ambulances, stretcher parties, walking wounded singly, in pairs, in trios, and all, like ourselves, taking advantage of the early morning lull. Dead horses, duckboards and ammunition lorries knocked cock-eyed by the night's shelling, viscous and often bloody scum floating on top of every shell crater – for every single shell crater, even the newest, was flooded.

The Colonel was at his best when visiting and talking to a battery under stress, and it was on such occasions that he showed his humanity. He was there to encourage as well as to command, and officers and men, though dazed with exhaustion, casualties, and lack of sleep, seemed glad to see him. It was as though he left with them some portion of his stout heart. He took practical steps too, and I fancy he was the first Group Commander to order his batteries to man their guns by reliefs, which enabled the relief not on duty to go to the back areas for a brief rest.

As for me, I was beginning to sense the subtle yet potent difference between the war in Gallipoli as I had seen it and the war in France and Flanders. In Gallipoli, at any rate during my time, morale could hardly have sunk lower; in Flanders, even during this present hopeless battle, it remained astonishingly high. I was, I think, becoming more perceptive in other directions too. Intensely moving though I found it to stand on the Ramparts beside our dug-out entrance in the comparative calm of a summer evening and watch some fresh Division march – usually in silence – through the Menin Gate on its way towards the line, it was more moving still to see its remnants marching back by the same road a week or ten days later. . . . If it be true that the seizure of Passchendaele – for to such microscopic proportions had the grandiose objectives of the Third Battle of Ypres now been whittled down – was planned mainly for the purpose of saving France and her armies from disintegration, and if Haig's unawareness of the conditions in which his troops were fighting was equally true, I can only say it was a pity he was not beside me at the Menin Gate. For had he witnessed with his own eyes the decimation of so many of his Divisions, he would surely have called a halt to this senseless and bloody struggle for the prize of a few more thousand square feet of mud.

CHAPTER V

Third Army Front

The end of September found us so spent that, like many others, we were transferred down south to the peaceful Third Army front, and there we were to rest and recuperate. We reported to IV Corps Heavy Artillery near Bapaume, from whom we received orders to proceed to Beugny, a flattened village on the Bapaume-Cambrai road, and take over from a Group which was under orders for the Salient.

On reaching Beugny we found we had, instead of the usual crowd of guns all on top of one another within a few square hundred yards, some seven miles of front and twelve guns, two of which were so worn that they were to open fire only in the event of real emergency.

It was indeed a rest. One could with equal safety motor to Amiens to buy butter and vegetables for the mess or ride out on horseback to look for the front line. We could go and dine with our neighbours without hearing a shot fired; a hostile shell was an event. There were partridges to be hunted – with the brigade car,[1] because we had an old Belgian shotgun but no dogs – over the barren fields round our headquarters. I remember, too, how one of our planes, unable to establish contact with the battery for which it was conducting a shoot, landed in the battery position and asked the battery commander if all his wireless operators were on leave, or only some of them.

But the war was not to be won in that way, and in late October we moved up towards Arras to join in a demonstration against the Hindenburg Line by Bullecourt. We silently returned to Beugny by night three weeks later, and thirty-six hours after that we were taking part in the dramatic

[1] Till the Colonel stopped it.

Cambrai show, a surprise attack by massed tanks without the usual preliminary artillery bombardment. It nearly succeeded; had it done so it would have been no mere local success. Our tanks broke through – the sounds of their assembly the previous night had been drowned by the spasmodic gunfire of our guns at entirely normal targets – and the break-through was so swift that neither the cavalry nor the exploiting infantry were close enough up to follow in time. The Germans, caught very much on the wrong foot at first, were thus able to recover their balance – trust the Germans for that! – and they counter-attacked so fiercely in Bourlon Wood that the tables were turned and our initial victory suddenly showed every sign of becoming a serious reverse.

During the German counter-attack we supported the hard-pressed 56th (London) Division with many COMRADES,[1] plastering Moeuvres and Inchy and Tadpole Copse with every gun we had. From the map-board it was clear we were nearly back at the start-line, and it was partly by our efforts that the enemy did not break through, as he did a few miles further south at Gouzeaucourt. It was a sad ending to a bold and cleverly conceived assault, one in which tanks were properly used for the first time, and in perfect tank-country too. Sadder still, the upshot was construed by some as yet another tank failure.

A much-needed reform in the organization of Heavy Artillery now came into being. Hitherto battery after battery had been passing through our hands, some to remain with us for as little as a couple of weeks, others for a month or two. The confusion and amount of paper work which all these changes caused was endless and made life as difficult for us as for the batteries. More unsatisfactory still, we did not get to know them nor they us. Now all this was to be altered. Henceforth we were to be known as a Heavy Artillery Brigade, and to us were allotted four batteries which were to remain with us, for better or for worse, till the end of the war. In the event four better batteries than Toc 1,

[1] See page 34.

Toc 2, Toc 3, and Toc 4[1] would have been hard to find.

Of the four, we had met only Toc 1 before. A 9·2 howitzer battery, they had found themselves in our Group during our brief Bullecourt sojourn in October: they were occupying a luxurious position in St Léger where they had been gaining notoriety and creating amusement – not in the Colonel's eyes – by their erratic shooting. It was not their fault; their guns were very worn. We remembered them for a second reason. Having stated they were much too short of men to provide a working party, the Colonel discovered thirty of their gunners hard at it constructing a tennis court for the use of their officers. In November they were uprooted from St Léger to join some other Group for the Cambrai battle, and when the Brigade was formed in December they came, a trifle sheepishly, to us. Just before Christmas we at brigade headquarters were sitting quietly at tea listening to them finishing off a 300-round shoot – their position was barely a mile away – when we heard a loud explosion followed by silence. Two or three minutes later their battery commander, Balfour, rang up to report a premature. The Doc and I went straight over in the car and found a number of ambulances and a great crowd of cold-blooded infantry sightseers standing in the road behind the guns. No. 4 and its entire detachment had been blown to pieces. No one discovered the reason. Some said the premature was due to a faulty shell; others – more probably – to road grit which had not been cleaned off and which exerted so much pressure when the gun fired that the walls of the shell gave way and the shell exploded instantly. Balfour died of pneumonia in hospital at Grévillers a short time later. Then, in the same week, the battery was re-equipped with six 9·2s of the latest mark capable of a range of twelve thousand yards, and Major Pargiter arrived to take command.

Toc 2, Toc 3, and Toc 4 were all 6-inch howitzer batteries, and they too had been ordered to the Beugny area for the

[1] Our private code names for 95, 244, 277, and 299 Siege Batteries R.G.A. respectively – 'Toc' being the army parlance for T, the initial letter of the Colonel's name.

Battle of Cambrai; they made and occupied sites in the fields around Morchies – in the middle of Morchies in the case of Toc 4 – and there they were when they joined the newly-formed brigade in December.

In January we went out of the line with our four batteries for a shake-down holiday at Gézaincourt, a pleasant village near Doullens. During our stay there the silence of the village street was shattered late one night by an uproar so violent that I picked up my revolver and roused the nearest N.C.O. – the Artillery Clerk – to help me in dealing with it. We ran out into the street and had our best laugh for months. The centre of the disturbance was a drunken gunner of Toc 1; in the moonlight he had mistaken the local priest for a girl. Since the priest was wearing his cassock and the time was long past midnight it struck me, if not him, that the mistake was understandable.

Our remaining ten days in Gézaincourt were free from incident, and the brigade returned to Beugny to take a frenzied part in the elaborate defensive preparations which were now being made along the whole of the Third and Fifth Army fronts. It was then that Toc 2, always an outspoken battery, complained they spent their time providing working parties for the Adjutant. It was true, but the Adjutant could not help it.

A few days after our return from Gézaincourt a battery armed with 6-inch Mark XIX guns arrived in Beugny and was placed under our command. This was 484 Siege Battery R.G.A., named by us Toc 5. They had just come out from England and were very green, so green that one night during their first week with us their portable forge was stolen by some other battery from the very middle of their gun position. I remember how angry the Colonel was when he heard of it – with them, and not with the thieves.

The Colonel now wanted the brigade to have a crest, and no one who knew him was surprised when he said it must be based on the theme of the Early Bird which caught the worm. I wrote to my artist uncle, and he soon sent the two birds which are reproduced below. The Colonel decided on the more contemplative one, ordered stencils and rubber stamps from somewhere in England, and it appeared on all the brigade's motor transport and letters till the end of the war.

The work of an Adjutant of a Heavy Artillery Brigade is difficult to define, depending as it does on the requirements and nature of the Colonel whom he serves. In my case I had to become as it were the Colonel's shadow, but I tried not to be a black or even grey one. In addition I made it my business to establish personal relations with our batteries and with their officers, because it did not seem to occur to the Colonel that this was necessary or even desirable. I established similar relations with my equals or juniors at Corps Heavies – Darby the Staff Captain, a good staff officer; Smithers the Ammunition Officer, pleasant and obliging; the various assistants in the Counter-battery office. Healing, the excellent Brigade

Major, was my superior, and I treated him with respect – in much the same way as the Colonel should have treated, but did not treat, Marshall the Brigadier-General. The Counter-battery Colonel, Loring, was shrewd and approachable; he and the Colonel got on well enough, if distantly. In short we always found Corps Heavies friendly and helpful. We thought them leisurely too, but what lesser formation does not think that of its immediate superiors?

Of my day to day work, I was responsible for keeping our batteries supplied with ammunition, rations, stores, and most replacements. I was also responsible for the smooth running of the brigade office, and for the pay, administration, leave, and welfare of the R.A. personnel of brigade headquarters; some of this I delegated to the Orderly Officer, Benwell. By now my Artillery Clerk was Corporal Fulton, who appeared earlier in this book as Bombardier Fulton.[1]

Numerically the strength of brigade headquarters was small, but since nearly every man was rated as a specialist of one kind or another there were cross-currents which at times had to be watched. We had three or four horses; I can remember only the purpose of Jenny, who drew the cable-cart. In spite of the shape of his legs the Colonel did not ride, even for exercise. I fancy he disliked horses as a species; he preferred motors and motoring but did not try to ride a motor-cycle.

For all of us at brigade headquarters there were periods of slackness as well as of pressure; a time of pressure I still remember occurred immediately after our return to the line from Gézaincourt, when the brigade was ordered to construct and maintain a number of reserve battery positions in

[1] See page 29. Since I needed a more competent Artillery Clerk than the one I found on becoming Adjutant, I asked Bdr. Fulton if he was prepared to take the job on, and my battery commander if he was willing to release him. Both agreed, and after some difficulty with the two Record Offices concerned he was at last transferred from the Royal Artillery to the Army Service Corps (Clerks' Section). He then had to become a Corporal instead of a Bombardier. The Colonel liked him from the start, and he proved a great success and remained with the brigade till the end of the war.

[46]

anticipation of the expected German offensive. As well as seeing that the batteries made them, it was my job to supply and deliver all the necessary materials – pit-props and elephants,[1] rabbit wire and duckboards, sandbags and corrugated sheets, camouflage, six-inch nails and one-inch nails, nine-by-three timber (for gun platforms, of which there were six at each position). The collection and delivery of all the items meant a continuous fight with Siege Park for lorries and still more lorries. Then I had to wring large working parties from aggrieved battery commanders, and at the same time implore Corps Heavies to send up less ammunition. Finally it was my personal responsibility to erect a board – made and painted by Gunner Freshwater, our brigade carpenter – at each position to enable inspecting Generals to know without being told that, for instance, the neat little notice H.A. 107 beside that wet hole partly covered by a corrugated sheet marked the command post of Heavy Artillery Reserve Position No. 107.

Of the general situation at that time, it was only too clear from the Order of Battle maps which reached us at regular intervals every few weeks that something was going to happen, and soon. These maps, beautifully produced by Army Printing & Stationery Services and compiled by the Intelligence staff of G.H.Q., covered the entire front and showed unequivocally that the bulk of the German and Austrian Divisions – all identified and named – were massed opposite the relatively short British front, which stretched for approximately a hundred miles from the Houthulst Forest (ten miles north of Ypres) to Barisis (five miles south of the River Oise).

The twenty miles of line north of the Houthulst Forest to the North Sea was held by the Belgians; it had been quiescent for several years and was likely to remain so because wide areas behind it had been deliberately flooded. For that reason the Germans would have gained little advantage by driving

---

[1] Sectional steel shelters, the forerunner of the back-garden air raid shelter.

them out. South of Barisis the French held the line as far as the Swiss border – say three hundred miles – and behind them the Americans as they arrived were grouping and training.

Long and in places vulnerable though the French-held line appeared from the map to be, the concentration of enemy divisions made it a certainty that as a start the Germans intended to attack the British and no one else.

CHAPTER VI

March 20 1918

Whatever may have been known in high places – and it has been stated that G.H.Q. foretold the exact day, time, and place – the truth is that we of 90th Brigade R.G.A. did not know on March 20 that the Germans were going to attack at 5 AM[1] the following morning. Nor did we know that our little sector was to be the spearhead of the German effort.

Rumour, of course, had been prolific during March, and hardly a day had passed without the Sergeant-major's store-keeper or my batman or Gardiner the Signals Officer being told, "The attack's coming off in the morning, but thank goodness not on our front," or, "It should have started the day before yesterday, but it was put off because the wind was blowing the wrong way." And the Colonel was some-times told much the same sort of thing by people old enough and high enough to know better. But he, being a wise old bird, was not as impressionable as some of us.

It was not until the evening of March 20 that it became apparent matters were coming to a head one way or the other. Just before supper a motor-cyclist arrived from Corps Heavies with a hurriedly prepared map of the German forward areas in our sector.

'What on earth are all those little black dots?" asked Gardiner jovially, peering over the Colonel's shoulder as he unrolled it.

"German guns in the open, my boy," the Colonel replied. "Spotted by the Flying Corps a couple of hours ago."

[1] In the 1914-18 war the 24-hour clock was rarely used. Time was given as AM and PM.

The following IV Corps Summary of March 20, which arrived with the map, shows how much – or how little – we knew:

IV CORPS SUMMARY OF INFORMATION NO. 95 20 MARCH, 1918

ENEMY INTENTIONS (*From Fifth Army sources*)

Recently captured prisoners of various units including the 107th Division, the 44th Pursuit Flights, the 414th Trench Mortar Company, and the 28th Foot Artillery Regiment were unanimous in predicting that the German offensive would commence in the next few days.

The prisoner of the 28th Foot Artillery Regiment states that the attack will be preceded by an intense bombardment, during the final two hours of which gas shells will be fired. Thereafter two hours will be allowed for the air to clear, and then artillery and infantry will advance simultaneously.

HOSTILE ARTILLERY ACTIVITY

Save for a few shells put into Demicourt today, hostile artillery has been very quiet.

A special reconnaissance of the area between Moeuvres and Inchy from 2.30 PM to 4 PM today reports a number of suspected new gun positions and material in the open, chiefly in the areas E 7 c and d, E 8 c, and E 13 b. No guns were actually seen, but objects covered by tarpaulins were observed. Accurate location was difficult owing to the clouds and the large number of objects seen.

ANNEXE TO IV CORPS SUMMARY NO. 95

Special examination of a prisoner of the 21st Bavarian Reserve Regiment, 16th Bavarian Division, captured near Bullecourt on night of 18th-19th March.

INTENTIONS

Prisoner states that a huge offensive was to be carried out on the front from Rheims to Bullecourt, but the main attempt to break through would be made at both extremities.

Orders had been issued that they were to be ready by noon on the 19th, but prisoner understood that the attack had been put off, presumably owing to the weather. He had no idea how long it would be delayed.

Prisoner stated that as the main opposition was expected from our airmen a considerable concentration of hostile aircraft had been made, including Austrian and Bulgarian units.

Austrian and Bulgarian artillery was also present on the front, also a large number of Austrian Volunteer Assault Troops.

He had no knowledge about tanks.

The initial assault was to be made by specially trained Assault Division, but prisoner was under the impression that his Division would also take part in the attack.

Prisoner admitted that he had been examined three times but that he was careful not to give anything away.

(*From Third Army Summary*)

Information obtained from a deserter of the 28th Reserve Infantry Regiment, 185th Division, who surrendered in our lines near Bullecourt on night of 17th-18th March.

CIRCUMSTANCES OF CAPTURE

Prisoner was on fatigue carrying duckboards to the enemy's front line. The line was thinly held and he seized upon a favourable opportunity to desert.

Prisoner is a Pole, born in March 1898, and was called up in October 1917. He has a strong dislike for the Germans and on the 8th inst. tried to desert back to Germany. Having reported sick, he went to Douai but was refused admission to the hospital; he thereupon took a train and succeeded in reaching Louvain via Tournai and Brussels; he was, however, arrested at Louvain on the evening of the 9th inst. and sent back under escort to his regiment on the 12th.

PREPARATIONS FOR AN ATTACK

The last few nights prisoner's company has been employed in carrying trench mortar ammunition towards the front line. The work was very heavy but the men were urged to do their utmost as the work was pressing.

TANKS

Prisoner has never seen any tanks or heard anything about

German tanks but he states that on the 15th, when on a day-light patrol, he had seen a notice-board on which was written 'Tank Stelle 7'. All the men were much surprised. Prisoner thinks the board is placed on a track which has been prepared for tanks as he noticed it had been to a certain extent levelled by shell holes having been partly filled in.

GENERAL

There is a great deal of talk about an impending offensive and a state of tension appears to exist amongst the troops. All sorts of rumours are current. The back areas are said to be full of troops of an Assault Division. Prisoner has no idea which this Division may be.

Several dates have been mentioned for zero day, the original date having been the 12th. Then the offensive was said to have been postponed to the 14th, then to the 18th.

Hindenburg, Ludendorff, and the Crown Prince are said to have been in Douai on the 12th.

His company commander told prisoner that an offensive was imminent and the men are being continually urged to hurry work and are made to work very hard. As regards details, prisoner states that no one but Hindenburg himself knows what is really going to happen, and he can only repeat rumours.

AUSTRIAN ARTILLERY

On the occasion whilst prisoner was on patrol and saw the 'Tank' notice-board, he also saw an Austrian artillery officer who asked his way to a battery. On the 12th in Louvain, while with his escort to return to Douai, prisoner saw three trains of Austrian artillery in the railway station.

RELIABILITY

Prisoner is a genuine deserter. He is very talkative and rather excitable, but, having only joined his regiment in January, he has little military experience and therefore is not in a position to form a critical opinion of his own.

CHAPTER VII

March 21

I awoke with a tremendous start conscious of noise, incessant and almost musical, so intense that it seemed as if a hundred devils were dancing in my brain. Everything seemed to be vibrating – the ground, my dug-out, my bed. . . . The great offensive had begun.

It was still dark. What time was it? I lit a candle. Just five o'clock. I seized the telephone beside my bed and buzzed up the exchange. "Any messages coming through?" I asked.

"No, sir."

"Then put me through to Tusculum."

"Mr Gardiner's speaking to them now, sir."

The door of my dug-out opened and in hurried the Colonel, clad in spectacles, pyjamas, and gum-boots. "Any report from the O.P.?" he asked.

"Gardiner's speaking to them now." As I spoke a terrific crash half lifted me out of bed. Out went the candle.

"Beside the clerks' dug-out," remarked the Colonel, peering down the road.

A wave of emotions now came tumbling into my excited brain. During the past few months and though we were barely five thousand yards from the front line, the war had seemed so remote that we might have been fifty miles away from it. No shell had fallen within a thousand yards of our headquarters, our batteries had been living in comfort and luxury, visits to O.P.s or trips up the line were as free from incident as a walk over the Yorkshire moors. Since the Cambrai show the whole brigade had suffered barely a dozen casualties. Indeed since Christmas life on the Bapaume front had been delightful – a succession of invigorating canters across the overgrown downs to the batteries, joy-

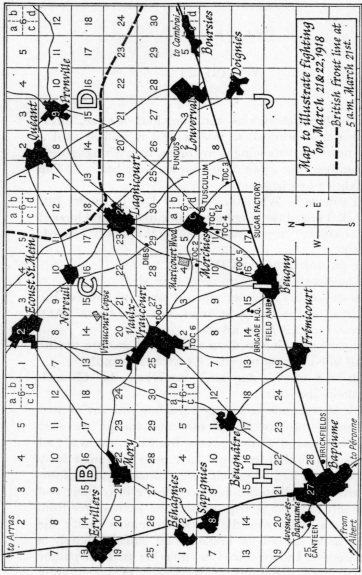

NOTE FOR THE USE OF THIS MAP: The large rectangles (lettered B, C, D, etc.) are divided into squares of 1,000 yards side, which are numbered 1, 2, 3, 4, etc. Each of these squares is divided into four sub-squares of 500 yards side, considered as lettered a, b, c, and d. (See Square No. 6 in each rectangle.) To locate a point within a sub-square, consider the sides divided into tenths, and find the point by taking so many tenths from W. to E. along the Southern side, and so many from S. to N. along the Western side; the S.W. corner always being taken as the origin, and the distance along the Southern side always being given by the first figure.

rides to Amiens through the snowy wastes of the Somme, early-morning partridge shoots over the fields around our headquarters.

All these happy memories came tumbling through my mind to be overwhelmed by this one tremendous fact – that a big shell had fallen in the roadway ten yards from my dug-out. . . .

The Colonel interrupted my train of thought. "Where are the S.O.S. orders?" he asked.

"In Gardiner's dug-out, sir. He was duty officer last night."

The Colonel hurried off. Big stuff was now falling all around us thick and fast, and I wondered how much longer it would be before my shack got a direct hit. The concussion was so continuous that it was impossible to light the candle. Suddenly the door blew off its hinges. Outside dawn was breaking slowly but surely, as if anxious to soften the vivid flashes of the shells which were bursting everywhere. Volumes of dust and smoke drifted past the doorway, blown this way and that by the fury of the storm. The fascinating smell of high explosives and ravaged earth drugged and bewildered me.

I do not know how long I remained in bed – it must have been nearly five minutes. I was trembling with excitement – or was it fear? – and I felt powerless to move. Besides, what was the use? There was nothing to do, and one might just as well be killed decently in bed instead of half naked while struggling into one's shirt. What a huge barrage they were putting down. All our lines must have gone during the first minute. Serve us right for not getting the Bury – a big buried cable system which Corps was laying – finished in time. No wonder the Germans lost Passchendaele Ridge if our barrages in the Salient last year were anything like this. Lord, that one was damned near! And what a stink, must be gas. What sort of a time are the batteries having? The infantry too. Pretty bloody, I suppose.

The human mind quickly accustoms itself to the most abnormal conditions. Within a very few minutes, so it seemed to me, I had been living in this inferno for years, and intense shell fire had become quite the usual state of affairs. A desire for action came back to me, and in the reeking semi-darkness I got out of bed and put on my clothes. The thought of survival hardly entered my head. Even if one was only wounded one would have precious small chance of getting away. . . . Though one might be captured. So better put on my new tunic, the one with the chevrons on it.

We had often discussed what we would do when the Germans launched their big offensive, and most of us had pictured ourselves lining the sunken road with – if you were lucky – one of the dozen rifles which our mobilization equipment tables allowed us. Well, here was the reality.

I put on my belt, fastened my gas-bag at the Alert, crept out into the roadway, and ran for Gardiner's dug-out.

"Every line has gone except the fool[1] one to Toc 6," the Colonel told me bitterly. "And thank goodness the bury from Toc 6 to Tusculum is still through."

"Any news from Tusculum?" I asked.

The Colonel handed me a pink-paper telephone message:

S.O.S. on Left Division front. All our batteries seem to have opened out. Tusculum.

It was now about twenty past five and quite light, though there was so much mist and smoke that it was barely possible to see a hundred yards. The shelling of our headquarters seemed to be over;[2] in front, however, the noise was greater than ever.

The Colonel went off to his shack to dress and I heard him shouting for his shaving water. I went outside again. Things had changed almost beyond recognition. The roadway was covered with earth, stones, and great lumps of turf. A dozen great shell holes, still smoking, gaped in the middle of the

---

[1] The ground line.

[2] During the advance several months later one of our batteries found a German map dated March 18 and on which our headquarters were marked as a Telephone Centre. The Germans must have thought, rightly, that twenty minutes concentrated fire would finish it off.

road, and all our beautiful telephone wires were trailing helplessly in the dirt. I climbed on top of the roadbank and saw new shell holes everywhere, hundreds of them. A big shell passed swiftly far overhead, bound for Bapaume or Achiet-le-Grand. I turned to watch the strafing of Toc 5, our 6-inch gun battery, who were firing merrily away half a mile in front. Jolly good, I thought, for they had been out only a couple of months and the enemy seemed to have them taped.

The Sergeant-major now appeared, walking smartly up the road, as spick and span as if he were going off on his weekly trip to the laundry at Albert. I noticed he too had his best tunic on.

"Jenny the cable-cart horse has been killed and the car's had a narrow escape, sir. The bottom half of the garage has been blown in but the car doesn't seem to have been touched. Thompson's trying the engine now. No casualties among the men – we've been lucky, sir. As soon as they've had breakfast I'll put them on to repairing the road."

"Right, Sergeant-major. Send all the men not on duty to the mined dug-out because there's no knowing when he'll start up again. Leave the remaining horses in the stable. They're as safe there as anywhere."

The office, a Nissen hut, was so perforated that it looked like a pepper-pot, and I noticed with resentment how one big shell splinter had come in exactly where I usually sat, embedding itself deep in my table. Since neither the Colonel nor I relished the idea of working there, we carried the map boards across to his shack, which at least had the protection of the roadbank.

The battle situation was so confused that for all we knew we might already be surrounded. Of what was happening in front we knew nothing. We were in touch with our immediate superiors, Corps Heavies, merely by wireless; we were out of touch with all our batteries except Toc 6, a detached section of Toc I, to whom we were through by means of a ground line over a mile in length and which strange to say kept through all day, and I do not know what we would have done without it. As previously mentioned, Toc 6 was in touch with Tusculum the brigade O.P. by means of a buried cable several feet underground.

The officer manning Tusculum now said there was too much mist and smoke to see anything, but that rifle fire was still incessant and German shell fire still very heavy, specially in Morchies – on the outskirts of which were Toc 1 and Toc 4.

Toc 6 were at the back of Vaulx. There was an infantry brigade headquarters of 25th Division five hundred yards in front of them, and the Colonel told Toc 6 to send an officer across for news. Throughout the day this infantry brigade proved one of our most reliable sources of information, but Toc 6 must have blessed us because each trip to the infantry meant running the gauntlet through the village, which was heavily shelled from dawn to dusk.

Almost daily and for many weeks past elaborate orders had been issued to us telling us what our batteries were to do when the Boche attached. These orders, with all their fresh targets and new rates of fire, became so complicated that it was next door to impossible to compete with them and with their numerous additions, amendments, additions to amendments, and amendments to additions. In the end Corps Heavies took pity on us, and on the eve of the battle issued a fairly lucid five-page document which, as the Brigade Major remarked to me, was positively the last word and contained all the winners.

Broadly speaking our artillery defence was divided into two phases, Counter-preparation and S.O.S.

Counter-preparation was intended to cramp the enemy's style as much as possible while he was massing for the attack; targets were such things as communication trenches, support trenches, or road junctions through which he was thought likely to go. But the moment he came over the top, all batteries were to switch to their S.O.S. targets – a barrage along the middle of No Man's Land. And since it had been realized that by this time communications would probably have gone west, equally elaborate instructions had been issued telling the batteries how to recognize the fateful moment. Judge the result of this thoroughness.

About an hour after the battle had started a wireless message arrived from Corps Heavies:

You should be firing Counter-preparation.

I rang up Toc 6 and asked them if they were. No, they were firing S.O.S. because from the heavy rifle-fire – vide para 3(a) on page 2 of Artillery Instructions XX – the Germans had already come across.

In the event the enemy did not leave his trenches till 8.30 AM, though it was later reported that his pioneers were seen soon after five o'clock standing upright in our wire and cutting lanes through it with wire-cutters.

The practical side of our defensive arrangements had not been neglected either. Since Christmas the front line system had been greatly strengthened, and a fine reserve line, known variously as the Haig Line and the Brown Line, had been dug about three thousand yards behind it. Unfortunately on our own front the Brown Line consisted only of a single wide trench; had there been a support trench the day might have gone differently because once our infantry were driven out of the Brown Line there was nowhere for them to rally for a counter-attack.

Our next defensive system was the Army or Red Line, which ran just behind our headquarters. It was merely an old German trench; consequently the wire was on the wrong side, and pioneers were working feverishly on it all day. Behind the Red Line there was nothing but the wastes of the Somme, and in the end this proved the most effective brake of all.

On the other hand artillery defences were far more thorough and complete. All existing battery positions had been wired in, an innovation in itself, and dozens of reserve positions and O.P.s had been made to cover both the Brown and Red Lines. Our brigade, as I have said, had been responsible for the construction of six of these reserve positions – one of which, to our disgust, was in the middle of our headquarters. Six gun-pits had had to be dug at each, wooden gun platforms laid and guarded from marauders, camouflage erected over each pit, command posts sunk in the ground and drained, and hundreds of rounds of 'juice' dumped on each position – and counted.

Such in a nutshell was the situation at seven o'clock on the morning of the twenty-first of March, when the Colonel and the Adjutant of the best Heavy Artillery Brigade in France sat in a shack at Beugny staring at the map board in front of them and wondering, each in his different way, what was going to happen next.

The skies hummed with planes, but owing to the low visibility there was little definite information they could give. From the number of W.P. zone calls – a signal used when hostile batteries are far too numerous to pin-point – they kept sending down, every map square behind the German lines must have been teeming with artillery. Indeed, as an R.F.C. observer remarked to me later, "In addition to every gun, howitzer, and trench-mortar from Central Europe, the Hun must have been using drain-pipes as well."

Suddenly an enemy plane made a spectacular and successful attack on a kite-balloon which was now rising a mile behind us. Flying very low, he circled round and round it, machine-gunning away for all he was worth. Out tumbled Tate, a balloonatic we knew. His parachute opened just in time, the ballon burst into flames and turned into a column of dense black smoke, the plane flew gaily away with every anti-aircraft battery and rifle within range – and many that were not – firing wildly at him.

A few minutes' later a 5·9 high-velocity shell came at us with a sickening scream and fell in the roadway near the garage. With one exception the men who were at work clearing up the road downed tools and scuttled for cover like rabbits. The exception was a gunner named Freshwater.

Gunner Freshwater, the hardest of hard workers and a

first-rate handyman, had one peculiarity. Unless desire for some essential such as leave or food or a new pair of boots compelled him to open his mouth and speak, he had not been known to say a single word to anyone during the year he had been with us. The Colonel, who was bad at remembering names, had once hailed him with, "Come here, carpenter!" Gunner Freshwater had taken no notice. The Colonel went close to him and said, "Didn't you hear me calling you?" Freshwater looked at him in his queer way and then said slowly, adding "sir" as an afterthought, "Yes, I heard you. But I'm not a carpenter. My name is Gunner Freshwater." He had one further eccentricity. When given a job to do, he would work like a horse till it was time for breakfast or dinner or tea or bed. But once one of those times arrived he would stop work suddenly, even if half way up a ladder with a sandbag on his back. Consequently Gunner Freshwater carried on when the shell fell.

"Get under cover!" roared the Sergeant-major, the only person from whom Freshwater was prepared to take orders.

Freshwater paused with his barrow in the middle of the road, and looked to see who was shouting. As he looked a second shell tore over our heads and burst with a rattling report at Freshwater's very feet. When the smoke and the dust had cleared away, we could see him lying dead on the road with his overturned barrow beside him.

Then that damned gun lengthened its range, and its third shot fell into the centre of the Field Ambulance at the bottom end of our road. Clouds of smoke, earth, and Nissen hut fragments rose high, and a few figures ran helplessly hither and thither among the huts and among the scores of loaded stretchers which lay around. The bombardment went on for a quarter of an hour, two or three shells a minute, some falling among the huts, some among the stretchers. It was like prodding an ants' nest with a stick, except that the ants were human beings and the nest a hospital.

Those German gunners would surely have shuddered had they seen the effects of their handiwork. Yet it is only fair to say they were probably shooting at the Cambrai road; it

was a sad mistake that a Field Ambulance should have been
sited so close beside it.

It was as well that there was little time for thinking about
such matters; at half past ten a dusty and panting runner
arrived from Toc 1 with a welcome and comforting message
from Major Pargiter:

> Still firing S.O.S. Normal rate. All O.K. here. Wireless gone
> west. Any fresh orders? Nothing to be seen from Tusculum,
> and Brigade[1] had nothing to report except Boches massing in
> front of Quéant.

We had no fresh orders; we gave the runner a drink and
sent him back with the news that all was well at Toc 6 and
that we knew nothing about the situation.

A few minutes later a runner arrived from Toc 2, sited
behind a desolate copse named Maricourt Wood midway
between Morchies and Vaulx. Toc 2 was commanded by
Aglionby – their battery commander, Major Lushington,
was on leave in England – and his message ran:

> Lines still down. Enemy fire persistent but slackening. Am
> Still firing Counter-preparation. No zone calls received.
> Wireless aerial damaged but still in action. No wounded or
> stragglers have passed here.

The last sentence was a just tribute to 6th Division. We
sent the runner back to Toc 2 with orders for them to switch
at once to S.O.S. targets.

The suspense was becoming unbearable. What was happening? Even the Colonel began to fidget; unexpectedly he
said to me, "Tell the Sergeant-major to get that horse of ours
buried."

I knew the Colonel too well to attempt to argue with him,
and I went out to find the Sergeant-major. When I told him
he looked pained but said nothing; ten minutes later I
strolled down to see how they were getting on.

He, Fulton, and half a dozen more were digging silently

---

[1] An infantry brigade headquarters of 6th Division living in palatial
dug-outs near Toc 1.

away. Shrapnel shells were whining over our heads and bursting with pretty white puffs over the Cambrai road a quarter of a mile away. The sight of a 1st Class Warrant Officer and six men burying a horse while the Germans were thundering at our very gates appealed to my sense of humour, and I took off my coat and helped them to haul poor Jenny into her grave. It must have been an unpleasant task for the Germans digging her up again and burying her properly, for her grave was only eighteen inches deep.

Toc 5 provided us with the only other comic relief of the day.

As I have said before, Toc 5 had been out only a few months, and during their first weeks the punctuality with which they sent in their daily peace-warfare returns left much to be desired. So it spoke volumes for the fear they had of me when at about five minutes past twelve a breathless officer arrived and handed me the Noon to Noon ammunition return. He saluted and said, "Major Austin told me to say he's very sorry if this is a few minutes late today, sir, but under the circumstances he hopes you won't mind."

During the past half hour the visibility had improved considerably; at ten minutes to twelve a telephone report from Tusculum told us that the Boche had managed to break through:

> Enemy advancing on Lagnicourt at 11.30. Numbers of infantry and cavalry and tanks on right of Pronville.

This was straightway telephoned back to Corps Heavies, with whom we were once more in fitful communication; the last part of the message must have caused fluttering in the dovecots because German tanks were then an unknown quantity.

Next a report arrived from our furthermost battery, Toc 3, occupying an exposed position two thousand yards in front of Morchies and just north of the Bapaume-Cambrai road. Toc 3 had sent the message to Tusculum, whence it had been telephoned to us. It was a relief to hear from them, but their news was alarming:

F.O.O. reports columns of men and horses advancing over crest in front of Fungus, and down valley and left past tanks over crest. Infantry in valley to left of O.P.

Fungus, so named because it had sprung up in a night, was a Forward O.P. near Louverval and manned that day by an officer of Toc 3. The middle part of the message was meaningless though it showed that the enemy had made another breach in our line. What infantry, I wondered, looking at the map board. Not Germans, I hoped, or Toc 3 would soon be surrounded.

Barely five minutes later a second and terser message arrived from Toc 3:

O.C. Battery wounded. Bengough and two O.R.s killed.

Bengough was an elderly subaltern, and orders had reached us that very morning for him to return to England for duty with the Ministry of Munitions.

Mills, the battery captain of Toc 3, was away doing an artillery course at Lydd. So with Major Sunley wounded – he had just been awarded an M.C. for rescuing an airman who had crashed by the front line – command of the battery now devolved on his subalterns, and I wondered what chance they would have of getting him back to the Casualty Clearing station.

Messages now began to come in fast. 'Dog', the code name for the infantry brigade near Toc 1, sent us a signal by some devious route, probably through their Division:

Situation does not appear satisfactory. We are still holding the reserve line D 25 a to J 2 b. Enemy batteries reported D 13 d 9.0 [*the old No Man's Land in front of Quéant*] some time back and D 26 b 7.7 [*well inside our old front line*] recently. Numerous Huns in Leech Avenue and Lynx Support D 26 b. Consider batteries and trench named in last para are your best targets. Pretty heavy fire would be appreciated.

So the enemy had now been able to get his artillery across No Man's Land and into action well inside our lines. Toc 3 were certainly outflanked and might by now be surrounded.

The message from Dog was immediately amplified by a message from Tusculum:

German line now in front of wire of reserve line. Get on to area D 26 a and b.

We ordered Toc 6 to sprinkle a dozen into D 26 a and b. Another appeal from Dog arrived, unhappily too late for us to help them. Timed 12.25, it did not come till 1.15:

Enemy now in great numbers in Louverval and advancing against our intact reserve line in D 26.

Next a badly-wounded runner struggled in with a letter from Major Clark of Toc 4, who were on the outskirts of Morchies. This was the first message we had had from them, and as we feared they had been getting it in the neck. Timed 12 noon and covered with bloody finger marks, it read:

Since my last message [*which we had not received*] my position had been very heavily shelled and I have only been able to keep in action at intervals. I have expended 200 rounds on Counter-preparation and S.O.S. and succeeded in getting off about 25 rounds on an enemy concentration in D 26 at the request of DOG. My F.O.O. [*who was manning one of the reserve O.P.s*] reports that the barrage at 11 AM was only heavy on the Left Division [*25th Division*] front. My battery is evidently under observation as directly I open fire I am engaged by about four 5·9 H.V. guns. My casualties are at present about 1 officer and 10 O.R.s wounded and 5 O.R.s killed.

Thus Dog's appeal had not been in vain.

A few minutes later another runner arrived, this time from Toc 1. He brought a note from Pargiter:

Attached is from DOG. I am engaging at their request the Hun battery at D 13 d 9.0 with one piece and the Strand with two pieces.

The attached message:

Huns at 11.45 advancing down valley J 2 b and in great numbers through Louverval towards the Cambrai road. So

E

[65]

far as we are concerned we believe the reserve line on 6th Division front to be intact, but to our right the enemy has got through reserve line and is advancing against Brown Line. I hear the Hun is in Noreuil.

At 1.12 Tusculum telephoned:

Much hostile artillery advancing along Pronville-Lagnicourt road. Germans concentrating at J 8 b.

J 8 b was only a thousand yards from Toc 3, and five minutes later Tusculum reported:

Germans advancing from J 8 b.

Next a belated message timed 12.50 arrived via Toc 6 from the infantry brigade at Vaulx:

Enemy reported to be digging in in front of Brown Line.

This was almost good news; the enemy must be held up or he would not be digging in.

A further note arrived from the skipper of Toc 2:

Wounded infantry N.C.O. (reliable) reports that we hold Brown Line. Wounded trench-mortar gunner (not reliable) reports enemy in Lagnicourt. Wounded West Yorks officer reports Boche held Travel Trench at 11.30, but the Essex were about to counter-attack. We bombed enemy half-way out of Leech Avenue.[1]

Our line to Toc 2 must have then been put through, for a telephone message was received from them:

DIBS [*the code name for an infantry brigade headquarters of 6th Division near Lagnicourt*] report that enemy are massing in eastern outskirts of Lagnicourt and that bombardment would cause great execution. I have engaged and repeated to Toc 1.

Ten minutes later Tusculum reported:

White rocket fired from Lagnicourt and enemy visible on western outskirts.

[1] Compare with first message from Dog.

The rocket must have been the signal of Lagnicourt's capture.

The next message showed that Toc 2 were having it hot:

We are running short of tubes, please give bearer 200. The Boche is in the sunken cross roads where DIBS are. We have just pushed him up the hill with our barrage and he has retreated to the cross roads again. Infantry now up to support.

I knew those sunken cross roads well; the Colonel and I had been to liaise with Dibs two or three mornings ago. I looked at the map and was wondering what had become of them when the telephone orderly ran in with perhaps the most dramatic message of all. Toc 6 had phoned it to us; it had been given to them by the pigeon loft near their position:

To 6th Division. We hold most of Bradford Reserve and Skipton Strong Point. All papers and plans destroyed. Boche are all round. We are manning road round brigade head-quarters. Shorten artillery barrage. DIBS by pigeon service.

We did not hear of Dibs again.

At three o'clock a signal arrived from Corps Heavies as if in answer to our unspoken thoughts:

No orders can be given for withdrawal of batteries at present. Batteries must hold on if possible. Any zone calls from the air should be answered if possible and also any orders from 6th Divisional Artillery.

The Colonel snorted. It was an insult to tell our batteries to 'hold on if possible,' and of course zone calls from the air would be answered if possible.

To us on the spot there seemed no doubt that the time had come to withdraw the heavy artillery in our sector, yet we recognized how difficult it was for the powers-that-be to make the decision. So many different factors had to be considered – the situation on the fronts of the Corps on our flanks, the supply of reserves, and the fact that it would soon be growing dusk. However it was plain that every five

[67]

minutes' delay would diminish the chances of getting our guns away.

At ten minutes past three a significant LL call[1] came down from the air:

1000 Fan C 14 d 8.0

This, interpreted, meant that German infantry were a thousand strong in Vraucourt Copse. Toc 6 for one answered the call; the range was under three thousand yards.

Between three and four o'clock there was a distinct lull as though both sides were licking their wounds, though the noise of rifle fire grew ominously nearer and nearer. A reserve battalion of 25th Division came up in artillery formation; several small parties crossed the roadway beside our headquarters. They were under no illusion as to the hell which lay a couple of thousand yards in front of them, and some looked enviously at us in our comparative safety.

At 4.25 PM two even more significant zone calls came down:

G.F. Art S.W. C 18 b 9.7 [*Fleeting Opportunity Target: Artillery moving south-west along Quéant-Lagnicourt road*] C 17 a 2.5 N.F. [*Battery now firing from just north of Lagnicourt*]

The next report – from Toc 1 – rushed our thoughts a mile or two further south, whence news of late had been scarce:

4.35 PM. Large bodies of Boche advancing up valley between Morchies and Louverval. Am engaging. Juice running short.

An hour later, just as the suspense was becoming unbearable, came the orders, welcome yet unwelcome:

Batteries will retire to reserve positions covering Brown Line.

"Not far enough," the Colonel growled. "The Boche will be on top of us again before we've been in action an hour or two."

Runners from all our batteries except Toc 3 were standing by; we sent them off in pairs with the orders. Bell of Toc 3 was manning Tusculum; we told him to try to get back to

[1] Special Opportunity Target.

his battery because we hoped there was still a sporting chance for them.

While the day's events were unfolding I had found plenty of work, but now I felt the least I could do was to go round the batteries to see how they were faring. So I sent word to Thompson to bring up the car, and told my batman to pack up my kit while I was away.

Thompson appeared, as imperturbable as ever, and off we went. It was nearly dark as we left our headquarters and turned into the Cambrai road. Complete and uncanny silence reigned save for the crackle of musketry away on the left. The ruins of Beugny, through which we were now driving, seemed strangely deserted. We sped on and on past the sad trees that flanked the road till we reached the cross roads by the sugar factory, its roofless walls grimmer and ghostlier than ever. We turned off towards Morchies.

Hatch, a very gallant subaltern who had won the M.C., D.C.M., and M.M., was in charge of operations at Toc 1; Major Pargiter had walked over to Vaulx to encourage Grainger, Badman, and Tuck at Toc 6. The big 9·2s were being dismantled, I saw. Their barrels had already been hauled on to their transporting wagons and the Cats (caterpillar tractors) were waiting in noisy readiness. Thanks to their fine deep pits Toc 1 had escaped with few casualties. In the early afternoon, they told me, the battery position had been sprayed by machine-gun fire, and Major Pargiter had given the signallers rifles and posted them on the bank on either side of the guns with orders to shoot at any Boche they could see. Everyone was working hard and in good heart, and I left them and walked on the few hundred yards to Toc 4, stumbling in and out of the many new shell holes on my way.

Till a week before the attack Toc 4 had been occupying a snug position in the middle of Morchies, but the Army Commander ordered all battery positions in villages to be moved – a wise precaution as it proved, because Morchies, always a sorry sight, now looked a mere shadow of its former self. Even in their new position in open fields Toc 4 had obviously had it worse than Toc 1, and their morale was noticeably lower too. Every square yard round them seemed to have been ploughed up by shell fire, and the whole area so reeked of Yellow Cross gas that I wondered how they had been able to carry on. One gun-pit had had a direct hit. Yet though the entire detachment – Fisher included – had been killed or wounded and though cartridges and fuses had been blown up galore, the how.[1] itself had hardly been damaged. I stayed with Toc 4 for ten minutes, they seemed glad to see me; I gave them such news as I could of the other batteries and went on my way with half a tumbler of neat whisky inside me.

Thompson had turned the car round, and we drove back to the sugar factory where I told him to go left towards Cambrai. Except for a few odd Jocks and a dead mule, the road, wide and straight, was deserted. I was wondering how close the Germans were when a kilted officer appeared in the roadway in front of us.

"Stop!" he yelled, brandishing a revolver. "Mon, where the deuce are you going?"

"To see what's happened to one of our batteries. Where's the Boche?"

"Aboot two hundred yards doon the road."

I told Thompson to turn the car round, stop the engine, and wait for me. Pleasantly warmed by the whisky, I grasped my torch in one hand and my revolver in the other and walked boldly on. Toc 3's side road was only fifty yards ahead. I pictured them pulling out under the very noses of the enemy; there seemed every likelihood of a scrap once the Germans heard the engines of their Four-Wheel Drives start up. I turned into the road in which their position lay: it was strafed to blazes. No F.W.D. would be able to pull guns

---

[1] 'How.' is an ugly word, I agree. But we called our weapon that, and rarely if ever 'howitzer.' Sometimes, as will be seen, we spoke of it as a 'gun,' which generically it was but technically it was not, and on occasions as a 'piece.' Hence the word 'how.' and 'piece,' whenever they appear in this book, mean either a 6-inch howitzer or a 9·2-inch howitzer.

away over such a surface. Toc 3 would have to blow them up and come away without them.

I soon reached the position. To my amazement the sunken road was absolutely deserted. The gun-pits were empty. I flashed my torch into the command post. Empty too, but for splashes of blood on the floor and a litter of field dressings.

I hurried back to the car; it was a mystery why Toc 3 had failed to let us know they had been able to get away.

"Seen anything of the Boche?" whispered the officer. "We've just got orders to dig in hereaboots."

"Then why not go to the sunken road where our battery was? There's plenty of wire just in front of the gun-pits and half a dozen good dug-outs."

"Right. Thanks . . . Good-bye."

"Good-bye," I echoed. "And good luck!"

Thompson gave the starting-handle a turn; the noise of the engine vibrated through the cold stillness with startling loudness. A burst of fire from a machine-gun which sounded less than a hundred yards away startled me out of my wits – it was so totally unexpected and hitherto everything had been so quiet. The bullets seemed to swish all round us. Thompson let in the clutch with an even bigger jerk than usual, the Vauxhall leapt away, and for the next mile he drove like a man possessed. Before the war he had driven a landaulette belonging to an old lady who lived near Manchester, and the Colonel often used to grumble because he drove so slowly. I wondered what the old lady would have said had she been with us now.

I got back to brigade headquarters to find a minor crisis had just occurred, in the form of a runner from Toc 2 with a note from Aglionby[1] saying his men were very tired and since he could not get horses with which to pull out his guns he would like permission to stay where he was for the night and pull out in the morning.

[1] We did not learn till later how magnificently Hugh Aglionby had fought his battery throughout the afternoon, and a detailed account which he wrote a short while before he was killed will be found in the Appendix.

The Colonel sat down and wrote a furious reply to tell him to pull out instantly; I sent off one of our own Don R.'s with a copy to make doubly sure he got it.

The Sergeant-major now came in to report that our two lorries were loaded up; we sent them off under the charge of Benwell, the Orderly Officer, to Bapaume Brickworks, which had been allotted to us as reserve headquarters.

Outside in the roadway there was considerable confusion. A battery of 60-pounders and the remains of a field battery had turned up; both claimed the pits beside our headquarters as their reserve position. After five minutes of argument, during which the beautiful horses impatiently pawed the ground as though the stupidity of human beings was beyond them, the 60-pounders gave way to the field and departed for a position further to the rear.

The field gunners then unlimbered their guns and set to work to lay out the line of fire; ten minutes later they were shooting madly away, though heaven knows what they were firing at. The O.C. of the battery – a subaltern – seemed so dazed that we took him into the mess and gave him a good meal. He was the only officer survivor of his battery, which had been in action in front of Toc 3 near Louverval. The Germans had overrun them early in the day, he said, but not before the gunners had twice repulsed them with Lewis guns and rifles. How they had managed to get any guns away he didn't know – only three had been fit to move and the other three were lying smashed on the position. After he had had something to eat and drink he improved in health considerably, and he climbed the roadbank twice to see if the enemy was in sight.

An officer of Toc 2 arrived to say that they had got all their hows. away except one which was hopelessly ditched in a shell hole. They had been able to borrow horses to try to pull it out, but only a tank could shift it. So, having removed the dial sight and breech block, they had left it.

Finally the Don R. who had been posted as a look-out on the Bapaume-Cambrai road came and reported that Toc 1's pieces had gone safely by.

[72]

It was long past midnight. All our batteries were well on the way to their new positions, and now there was nothing to keep us. The car was summoned, and the Colonel and I drove away from the shacks which had been our home for over six months. It was a painful moment, and when I looked back and saw the vivid flashes of the field guns firing away in the midst of our once spotless headquarters it seemed – as indeed it so nearly was – the beginning of the end of all things.

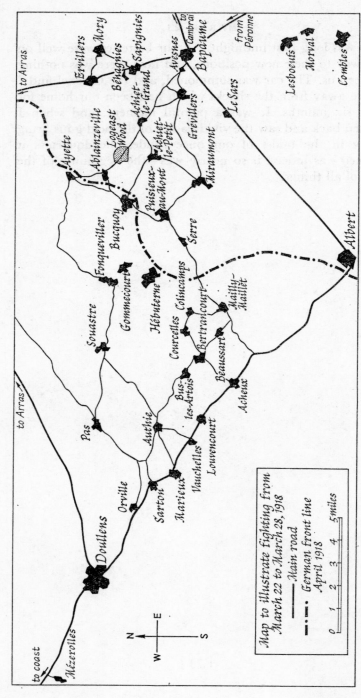

Area of Brigade's retreat, March 22—28

CHAPTER VIII

March 22

All that was left of the Brickworks was a series of stout brick vaults which had been allotted to another artillery brigade in addition to ourselves. The other brigade, having got there first, had occupied the best vaults and left us with the ones facing the enemy. We were far too weary to worry about such a trifle. My batman had kindly rigged up my bed but the Doc was sleeping in it, and I turned in on the floor. Considering that the Brickfields had been occupied during the past year by the A.S.C., the standard of comfort was very low; the vaults were atrociously damp and they also stank.

I slept intermittently till 5 AM, by which time I was so fed up with people stumbling over me that I got up.

The battle re-opened at daybreak.[1] Gardiner had been performing deeds of valour during the night and we were through by telephone to all our 6-inch how. batteries, all of which were in action once more in the fields north of Frémicourt. The Olympians had wisely decided that a moving battle was no fit place for such sluggish creatures as 9·2s. Consequently Toc 1's and Toc 6's pieces were now crawling across the Somme en route for the very back of the front; their officers and gunners were detailed off to reinforce Toc 2, Toc 3, and Toc 4. Toc 5, whose 6-inch Mark XIX guns were far less mobile than 6-inch hows., were still pulling in south of Frémicourt. Like the 9·2s, however, they too were withdrawn a day or two later.

I do not remember much of the incidents of the day.

[1] Extract from *Third Army Intelligence Summary* of 21.3.18: "The enemy apparently attacked this morning with eight fresh divisions on the front between Canal du Nord and Fontaine. . . . It is to be anticipated that ten divisions, possibly including the four originally holding the front, will continue the attack tomorrow."

During the morning the Colonel went off round the batteries, leaving me to talk to Corps Heavies, with whom we were once more, unfortunately, in perfect communication, and targets came through in shoals. The Major of Toc 1, very fed up about his 9·2s, came to suggest that the other batteries of the brigade, instead of borrowing his officers and men, could each lend him one of their hows. so that he could form a three-gun battery and carry on the good work. The Colonel at once agreed to this most practical proposal, and Toc 2, Toc 3, and Toc 4 were each ordered to hand over forthwith one how. complete with stores. Major Pargiter also wanted to take a party back in a lorry to try to salve his firing beams – massive steel girders on which 9·2s are erected – which they had been compelled to leave behind owing to lack of lorries, but it was a six-hour job to dig them out, and since the Germans were already in Morchies the Colonel would not hear of it.

As an example of what an Adjutant is expected to know and to do, the following note arrived from one of our batteries; the runner who brought it said he had been told to wait for an answer:

> We have taken up two pits at the approximate position you gave us but they are not numbered 267 so our map board is no use. We have received 200 rounds of ammunition minus the tubes. What is to be my Centre Line? A map is required. Where are we to run telephone wires to? I have no wire at all. I have no rations on hand for today.

Throughout the day the Germans advanced slowly but surely. Vaulx fell, and in the afternoon we heard that the infantry was fighting around our old headquarters in Beugny. Luckily we were still unaware that on our immediate right Fifth Army was in full retreat.

During the afternoon Toc 3 and Toc 4 performed a feat which earned them a mention in *The Times*.[1] Major Clark,

[1] From *The Times* of March 29 1918: "No troops could possibly have behaved better than the gunners, and in this I would especially say that I do not mean field gunners alone. The Royal Garrison Artillery has borne itself magnificently. The strain upon the men with the heavy

observing from a crest a few hundred yards in front of his battery, engaged the Germans pouring out of Vaulx at a range of about a thousand yards. I met him soon afterwards riding back on his Douglas to look for a new position. White with excitement and lack of sleep, he told me he saw his shells cutting great lanes in the enemy ranks as a scythe mows down grass.

One scene is fixed indelibly in my mind's eye. I was standing on a high bank which commanded a fine view up the Cambrai road as far as Frémicourt. The light was just beginning to fail. Batteries were in action all round; even the distant fields sparkled with countless tiny flashes. A heavy barrage was bursting on the far ridge. Along the road a slow stream of traffic was moving towards Bapaume and beyond, first waves of the tide which rolled westwards for days and days. Here and there a battery in column of route, walking wounded in twos and threes, an odd lorry or two, a staff car carrying with undignified speed the dignified sign of Corps Headquarters, a column of horse transport, and a biggish batch of German prisoners captured by 51st Division. The procession reminded me of a film; it was with something approaching a shock that I realized everything was in retreat.

Rumour was busy. It was said that the enemy cavalry was actually in sight, first on the far ridge towards Vaulx, next coming over the crest of the Cambrai road. People turned their heads and stared curiously into the distance, but there was no panic.

I stood watching the unforgettable scene for ten minutes; it was too sad for words.

The reserve ammunition dump of Corps Heavies was situated hard by, and I was joined by Shore, a subaltern of Toc 1, who a fortnight earlier had been put in charge of it.

---

guns has been stupendous, and their endurance, their resource, and their courage have been beyond all praise. . . . Two batteries of six-inch howitzers, near Morchies, completely broke up a heavy German attack. One battery, firing from the open at 1000 yards range, and the other from cover at 1700, got on to masses of Germans trying to advance and completely broke them up, and the attack utterly failed" . . .

When I had last seen him he couldn't say too much about his job – there was nothing to do; he was messing with the A.S.C.; never before had he had such quantities of strawberry jam and kidneys. But times had changed and he must have been watching the retreat with mixed feelings; Corps Heavies had just ordered him and his men to hold on "for the present," and five minutes later his telephone line back to them had gone 'dis.' I left him practising rapid-loading with his revolver; half an hour later his dump was set alight by a stray shell and he had the unpleasant job of trying to put it out.

In the late afternoon we got orders to move our batteries into positions in map-squares H 26, i.e. half a mile west of Bapaume. Corps Heavies were still in their old quarters at Grévillers; the Colonel decided we ourselves should go there too since Corps Headquarters were moving out and there was sure to be plenty of superior billets to let.

We loaded up our lorries once more and beat it through Bapaume, which was being strafed by a very big high-velocity gun. Needless to say the Albert road corner, usually so crowded with infantry officers patiently awaiting a lift to Amiens, was deserted save for a solitary Red Cap clad in a tin hat and directing the traffic. The Casualty Clearing Station just outside Grévillers was being evacuated. A fleet of buses stood outside – incidentally stopping all traffic – and nurses and wounded were clambering up on top. They were going to Albert, I was told.

When we reached Grévillers we found that all the best billets had been snaffled by the infantry, and we had to take possession of a miserable hovel beside the ruins of the church. Barely a hundred yards away Corps Heavies were still living in a suite of luxurious Nissen huts on top of the hill.

The Colonel and the Orderly Officer went off in the car to reconnoitre new battery positions; I went up the hill to see the Staff Captain about rations and ammunition supply.

As I climbed up the broad duckboard path which was neatly covered with strips of rabbit-wire to prevent you from slipping, I felt even more like a tramp than usual. The lawn

[78]

was as trim as ever; the garden, fringed with its decorous row of huts, had never looked in better shape. In the middle of the lawn stood the trophy, a German pip-squeak resplendent in its new coat of paint. Above it on a line dangled a row of magpies shot by the Reconnaissance Officer with the Brigade Major's gun. Sleek and gentlemanly clerks, carrying papers and what not, hurried in and out of the offices. Even the huts with their tarred and sanded roofs, daintily camouflaged ends, and sedate notice boards eyed me askance. I entered a hut labelled AMMUNITION OFFICER where friend Smithers told me – um, yes – that 6-inch ammunition was very scarce owing to the large amounts which had been dumped on reserve positions and – er – handed over to the enemy. However there were a few thousand rounds lying at Puisieux; we could draw from these if we liked – um, yes – but they weren't likely to be in very good condition because they had been salved nearly a year ago from the Somme. Failing that we would have to send our lorries fifteen miles back to the railhead at Acheux, where ammunition was being sent up as fast as possible; it wasn't considered safe to bring trains any closer to the line – um, yes – under present conditions.

I visited the Staff Captain next. Rations were to be drawn from the railhead at Achiet-le-Grand, which was being evacuated. Everyone could take as much as was wanted, he said, and indents were no longer required.

Then I went into the Counter-battery office, where you could always rely on hearing the very latest news. A clerk was packing a typewriter in the outer room and looked at me in surprise when I asked if anyone else was in. "Oh no, sir, it's dinner time," he said. "They're all in the mess having dinner."

I went to the mess hut round two sides of the lawn – crossing the grass was forbidden – and saw the whole of Counter-battery staff sitting in candle light at a big table with Colonel Loring at the head. I announced my presence by wishing him good evening, and the Orderly Officer greeted me with an affable smile and asked me to sit down and join them. I replied I was sorry I hadn't time.

"Find time for a drink instead," he said. "And excuse candles – our electric light plant's being packed up, you know. Beastly nuisance shifting, don't you think?"

So I sat down and passed an enjoyable ten minutes hearing how Major X and his battery had been captured intact – an unfounded libel, but amusing if you knew Major X – and how the Americans were landing in thousands, and how we had attacked up north on a vast scale and captured Lens and Ostend, and how none of the big mines in the Cambrai road had been blown because the safety-keys were kept in Demicourt and by the time the sappers had sent for them Demicourt had been surrounded and captured. And, more truthfully, how Y Brigade had lost more than half its guns, and how poor A and young B and old C and many more besides had been killed.

We discussed the unaccountable silence of the German artillery on the night of the 21st, and why, even granted they were busily engaged in moving forward their guns, they had not made use of their long-range railway pieces. Two or three 9·45 H. Vics dropping shells on the Bapaume-Cambrai road could have made all the difference; as things were everything had been able to get away undisturbed. And what a difference it would have made, too, had we on our side had a couple of 6-inch guns snugly dug in at the Bapaume end of the Cambrai road and firing away down it, for it ran straight as a die for miles and miles.

After a final whisky and soda I crept back to our hovel, wrote and dispatched a few letters to our batteries, and so to bed.

Colonel Thorp, an idealized portrait. He looked very different when wearing steel-rimmed spectacles and a much older and shabbier cap

The author in January 1917

BEFORE

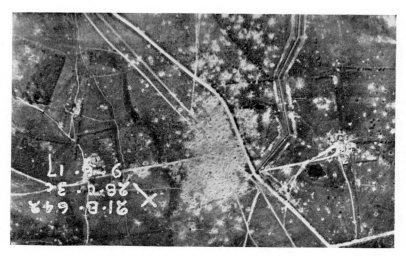

AFTER

Before and After: the effect of 290 rounds fired by a heavy
battery at a German battery emplaced beside the Yser Canal,
Ypres. Photographed by 21 Squadron R.F.C. on June 2
and 9 1917

CHAPTER IX

March 23

"Wake up! Wake up!"

I stirred drowsily.

The Colonel shook me. "Wake up!" he said abruptly.

Still half asleep, I sat up rubbing my eyes. It was quite dark. The atmosphere of the room was thick; the Doc and the Signal Officer were snoring softly on the floor beside me. Outside, but far away, I could hear the galloping noise of heavy gunfire.

"What's up, sir?" I asked, closing my eyes again and nodding.

"Read this." The Colonel thrust a message form into my hand and switched on his electric lamp.

Something in his tone roused me. I looked at the paper and read with dismay:

> The enemy has broken through at Mory. We have no troops left to put in the line. Sixth Corps.

That was all. I remember the despair I felt. The Colonel was lacing his boots. "Wake up the others and tell them to dress," he said. "Tell an officer of each battery to stand by the phone. I'm going to Corps Heavies to see what they are going to do."

"Did the message come through them, sir?"

The Colonel nodded, took his lamp, and went out.

I woke the others and told them the news; we dressed silently and I think we half expected the Germans upon us that very minute.

I stood by the doorway watching and listening. Away to the north-east the guns were pounding and the sky was flickering incessantly. Around Grévillers everything was still.

Suddenly a great flash lit up the night – a 60-pounder battery at the end of the village had opened fire. Its shells tore through the cold night air with a hollow blasting roar; the ruins echoed and re-echoed; a flock of startled birds rose from the church and wheeled and wheeled again over my head. A 6-inch how. battery just in front opened up. What were they shooting at, I wondered. And what was happening? Then I saw the light of the Colonel's lamp coming back down the duckboard path.

"It's only an S.O.S.," he said scornfully. "Corps Heavies are trying to find out who sent that message – someone ought to be shot. We've just spoken to Sixth Corps. The Guards Division is in the line at Mory. Are those officers on the phone?"

The Colonel took up the receiver. "Who's that? Officer, Toc 4? S.O.S. on the Corps on our left; take down this target. Mory, M-o-r-y. Damn it, M-O-R-Y! Yes, Sheet 57 c, Beer twenty-one. Yes, anywhere in Mory. Get them off as quick as you can. Come on exchange, give me Toc 3 now!"

After breakfast the Colonel and Gardiner went off in the car round the batteries, and I was spending the morning in the office vainly trying to discover how much ammunition they had on hand when I suddenly heard the sound of bag-pipes and drums and ran out of doors to see what was going on.

It was magnificent and too moving for words. No music, not even the trumpets of the French cavalry which I heard screaming their wild song of triumph after the armistice, has stirred me as deeply as the sobbing, skirling pipes of the 51st Division playing their survivors back to the battle, and I shivered with pride as I stood there watching those grim Highlanders swing by – every man in step, every man bronzed and resolute. Could these be the weary, dirty men who came limping past us yesterday in ragged twos and threes, asking pitifully how much further to Achiet-le-Grand?

Who could behold such a spectacle and say that the pomp and circumstance of War is no more?

[82]

A little later a note came from the Major of Toc 1, going strong with his three borrowed 6-inch hows.:

Am still firing on Mory, keeping well clear of the line you ordered though I think we are now behind it. Have only about 25 more rounds per how., also no lorries. Can fill up with F.W.D.s if necessary, and I have sent to see if there is any six-inch how. ammunition in Achiet-le-Grand. I have now my three F.W.D.s, but should like a few lorries if possible.

Lorries, lorries, lorries! The cry was always for more lorries, but we could do nothing to help him. Corps Heavies had detailed all they could lay hands on to go off and fetch ammunition from the railheads.

During the morning Corps Heavies moved out of their headquarters, and we gratefully moved in. I could not help noticing that despite the shortage of lorries they were doing themselves pretty well. Lorry after lorry rolled up to be loaded with such delightful etcetera as the electric lighting set, arm-chairs, and a fine kitchen range which certainly had not been paid for by its present owners. Even the trophy went off tied to the back of a lorry; its gaily-painted little wheels twinkled round so fast that it looked like a toy.

I opened our office in what had been the Brigade Major's and prepared to relax for a while in the unusual comfort of our surroundings when a welcome visitor arrived.

Captain Gilbanks A.S.C – 'Gilly' when you knew him as well as I did – commanded the 'Cats,' Four-Wheel Drives, and hundred lorries that belonged to us – or, as he would always have it, that are merely attached to you, old dear – and he commanded them very well. Immaculate and well-groomed under even the worst conditions, he bore a very slight resemblance to the German Crown Prince. One of his ears was a little torn; he had done this by crashing in a shell hole while motor-cycle racing round the Arras track in early 1917. His recreations were collecting and wearing light-coloured breeches and any form of motoring, and his clubs included the Sixth Corps Officers' at Béhagnies and the

Army & Navy Leave Club in Paris – of which he was apt to say regretfully he was only a country member.

"Hullo, B.," he said. "Busy? Where's the Old Man?"

"No, not very. He's out, thank goodness. So what about a small spot?"

I poured out a couple of gins, and after discussing things in general I said that the Old Man had had a good idea – if no one else had thought of it first – and wanted a lorry sending to the ration dump at Achiet-le-Grand, now being evacuated, to pick up as much rum as possible and dish it out to the batteries, who'd no doubt be glad of it during the next few nights. "And don't forget to leave a jar or two here," I concluded.

"Righty-ho, old dear. It shall be done."

The sequel came late that evening, when my phone buzzed and the operator told me O.C. Toc 1 wished to speak to me.

"Adjutant here, sir," I said sleepily.

"Is that you?" Major Pargiter asked in colder tones than usual. "You know those rum jars you kindly sent us this afternoon?"

"Yes, sir," I replied, and added politely, "You mean the ones the Colonel told you not to open till we get on the move again?"

"Yes, but that's not the point."

"No, sir?"

"The point is that they don't contain rum. They contain Nut Oil for Chinese Labourers."

And the remarkable thing is that during the next hour Toc 2, Toc 3, and Toc 4 all rang up to make the same complaint.

The Colonel and Gardiner came back about noon, and Gardiner burst excitedly into the office to tell me that Toc 2, in action in the grounds of Bapaume Canteen, were running the canteen as well.

"The E.F.C. people are clearing out and wanted to set the place on fire but Aglionby wouldn't let them," he went on, his face one big grin. "He's put his B.Q.M.S. in charge and told him to give everything away. Have a cigarette." He tossed me an unopened tin of fifty De Reskes. "We've brought back a case of bubbly, two cases of whisky, and umpteen boxes of Coronas. The Colonel says you can have the car, and you'd better go before it's too late."

The news was spreading fast, and as Thompson and I were starting the R.S.M. came running out of his billet, buttoning up his tunic and shouting, "May I come too, sir?"

It did our hearts good to see the happy faces we met on the way. Every lorry driver had a pile of cigarette tins on the seat beside him. Every infantry soldier had his pockets bulging with them. Even the walking wounded had their arms full. Everyone was laughing.

The scene outside the great canteen was memorable; it might have been Christmas Eve.

On the grass in front of the marquees Toc 2's howitzers, drawn up in line twenty yards apart, were firing steadily away, one round per battery per minute. Across the road I saw a party of Toc 2's gunners with their tin hats at rakish angles; they were posing for the Official Photographer.[1] I looked round again at the line of guns, and saw a No. 2 pull the lanyard with a long Pantello in his mouth and a bottle of Bass in his free hand.

The officers of Toc 2 were lunching in an outhouse and had reached the sweets course – before each one of them was set a big open tin of peaches. A confused medley of hilarious, hostile, and welcoming shouts greeted me; when the noise had died down Aglionby invited me to sit beside him and gravely offered me the choice of lime juice, whisky, gin, beer, stout, champagne, wincarnis, port, benedictine, and crème de menthe.

I chose champagne, and when the bottle was empty Aglionby said they had been finding it as much as they could do to keep their soldiers on the guns. "Would you care to come and have a look?" he asked.

---

[1] Sir Philip Gibbs, I believe. At any rate, whoever he was, Toc 4 later in the afternoon put him under arrest for being in possession of a camera.

We walked past the howitzers into the biggest marquee. The mob inside was growing unruly, and the Quartermaster-sergeant of Toc 2 and his assistants seemed unable to cope with the rush. At least half a dozen men were climbing over the counters; a dozen more, already across, were pulling down stacks of tins and piles of boxes to see what was on top. It was clear the place was getting too popular. "Help yourself while there's time," Aglionby suggested gloomily.

An E.F.C. attendant came up and said to him in the confidential tones of the slightly drunk that he was going now and there was no objecshun at all the lads helping themselves because far better they got it than the 'Uns, but would he pleash purra guard over the whisky or theesh chaps won't be 'alf blind?

On the way back we examined our spoils. The Sergeant-major had a case of tins of café au lait, 9 large tins of biscuits, and 5 pounds of tobacco. I had 700 cigarettes, six dozen Gillette blades, one Ingersoll watch, one patent combined tin-opener and corkscrew, one whole roast chicken, two bottles of Grand Marnier, and one smallish package which, on investigation, was found to contain 144 boxes of Beecham's Pills. At a guinea a box these would have been worth £151 4s.

A noisy luncheon party was in progress in our hovel. The menu:

> *Prawns in aspic*
> *Cold boiled ham*
> *Pineapple with tinned cream*
> *Pol Roger '06*
> *Johnny Walker*

". . . Yes, I've always been a pretty good hand at choosing battery positions," I heard the Colonel saying with a chuckle.

The afternoon passed uneventfully. Corps and Corps Heavies had now gone from Grévillers, and when the Colonel saw how much room there was in the village and how all the men's huts were fitted out with beautiful wire beds, he told me to tell the batteries that if they liked they could each send a party of fifty men back for a good night's rest.

Night fell. It was cold and starry, and when the moon rose conditions would be perfect for bombing.

The Sergeant-major came into the office. "These parties from the batteries have all arrived, sir," he told me. "I've handed over six Nissen huts to them, but some of the men prefer to sleep underground in the big dug-out. And there's a big party of reinforcements for the brigade just turned up, sir. There's no nominal roll with them. Will you keep them here tonight and post them to batteries in the morning?"

"Yes, Sergeant-major. You might make out a nominal roll, and —"

CRASH!

God, what was that? We both ducked blindly. Huge splinters burst through the hut, travelling with incredible speed. Outside the branches were snapping off the trees as though torn down by a hurricane.

For fifteen seconds almost complete silence reigned through the camp. It was broken only by the noise of falling stones and branches. Then a piteous chorus of moaning and shouting was heard, and the Sergeant-major ran to the door and looked out.

"It hit the hut where I put the reinforcements," he said.

One can hear a howitzer fire, and one usually has time to dart for cover or otherwise prepare oneself; one can also hear the sharp distinctive bark of a high-velocity gun several seconds before the arrival of its shell. But this gun had given us no warning at all, and its shell had landed in our midst with the suddenness of a flash of lightning. What was it? we asked each other.[1]

The casualties inflicted by that one shell were high. Apart from fifteen killed and wounded, others were so completely blown to pieces that they could not be identified nor could

[1] Counter-battery told us later it was a 9·45 gun on a railway mounting, firing from the railway somewhere near Havrincourt at a range of about ten miles.

the number be determined. Many weeks later we received a letter from a woman in England asking if we could give her any news about her son, from whom she had not heard since he sailed to France. She had written to the R.G.A. Base Depot and been referred to us; the Depot had told her that according to their records he had been despatched to our brigade on March 20 in company with a draft of 40 other men. How could one adequately reply to her letter and tell her that her son was one of those blown to pieces?

As an example of how closely the tragic is allied to the grotesque, Bdr. White, the brigade medical orderly, told me that to him on that occasion the most horrible sight of all was that of an unwounded but frightened reinforcement whose bully beef tin, driven inwards hard by a shell splinter, had burst and scattered its repulsive-looking contents over his bare stomach.

Something had to be done, and quickly, for the wounded. It was impossible to telephone for ambulances because all the lines had gone, and I said I would go off to the Casualty Clearing Station and bring one. Fulton said he would come with me.

The Doc and Benwell and the Sergeant-major and several more set to work to dress the wounded. Gardiner and his linesmen went out to get the lines through again, and the Colonel was walking about as if nothing had happened.

Fulton and I put on our tin hats and hurried off. It was not a pleasant walk. A second shell fell short just as we were starting, and seemed to land exactly where we were going.

It had. On the road a hundred yards from the church gaped a monster hole six yards across and deep in proportion. Half in it lay a headless dispatch-rider; the petrol from the twisted tank of his motor-cycle was sizzling on the hot cylinder.

We hurried on. A third shell tore over our heads with a rush like that of an express train and burst on the hillside, but well short of our camp. "That's just about where our linesmen will have got to," Fulton remarked. The splinters seemed to travel for hundreds of yards, and we both fancied we had seen the flash of the gun in the eastern sky.

The C.C.S. was still being evacuated; there were plenty of ambulances, but at first it was impossible to get hold of one. An R.A.M.C. Staff-sergeant who was marshalling them told me I couldn't have one without permission from his Commanding Officer, and I wandered through the crowded wards in search of him. They reeked of blood and chloroform and iodine; the cries and groans of the wounded mingled with the too frequent crashes of the five-nines bursting close outside. Several field batteries were now in action just behind; as they fired the hospital huts shivered and shook continuously. At last I got my chit; the R.A.M.C. Staff-sergeant gave me an ambulance and shouted to the driver to be back as quick as he could. Off we went.

The driver drove mechanically. His face was white with dust, his eyes were bloodshot and half closed. We swerved round the big shell hole; the driver saw the dispatch-rider and pushed out his clutch as though about to pull up. "Dead!" I shouted; he nodded and drove on.

Close beside the church the Sergeant-major and a small party were waiting with the stretchers, which we handed in quickly and carefully.

"Right away, driver, and come back for another load!" The R.S.M. was always at his best at times such as this.

The 9·45 had not fired again, and we were hoping that its gunners were packing up in preparation for a forward move. But our hopes were dashed for soon after midnight it fired six more rounds into the village, and at daybreak three more.

German planes were humming overhead all night long, and bombs were dropping north, south, east, and west. It was the worst and noisiest night yet, and we all thought it heralded a tremendous new attack in the morning.

CHAPTER X

March 24

But, strange to say, next day there was a distinct pause; on our front at least the Germans seemed to have temporarily overreached themselves.

The battery resting parties returned thankfully to their batteries, and during the morning we heard that things were going very badly down south and that another big retreat right back across the Somme and the Ancre was likely. I think people were almost relieved to hear this; the country where we were now was so utterly waste that anything seemed better than settling down there for the months of trench warfare which would inevitably follow.

We prepared for whatever might turn up by sorting all the stores we had brought with us and dumping all the rubbish. The Colonel ever after swore that the Sergeant-major had loaded up the rubbish and dumped the rest; it certainly was remarkable that for months afterwards whenever we asked the Sergeant-major for anything at all out of the ordinary he would invariably reply, "That was left at Grévillers, sir – Colonel's orders!"

I did my bit by leaving behind for the Germans a pair of old gumboots in which I had set half a dozen drawing-pins, pins upwards, but afterwards my conscience pricked me for fear that some of our infantry had tried them on first.

After lunch we set to work to burn all the maps and papers we could find in the offices; it was remarkable how much Corps Heavies had managed to accumulate. Suddenly someone shouted. "Look! X. Don's[1] on fire!"

We rushed out; it was true.

[1] The familiar code name of the enormous ammunition dump which stretched for half a mile along the Bapaume-Arras road.

From our hill top we had a wonderful view. Through our glasses we could see men running about among the flames and smoke, but whether they were trying to run away or put it out or set it alight (so as to prevent the Germans from getting it) we had no means of knowing. If the last they were certainly successful, for withing five minutes X. Don was a fearsome sight. A huge column of grey smoke had ascended nearly half a mile into the sky; at the top it was spreading out like a vast mushroom. The dump crackled continuously; from where we were it sounded like thousands of sausages in a frying-pan.

We passed a pleasant and interesting quarter of an hour listening to the crackling and trying to guess the identity of the various things that were going up – rifle ammunition or Flying Pigs or Duchesses or Mills bombs or Stokes or shrapnel shells or H.E. The fuses went up like golden rain, and we had a really first-class thrill when a dump of Very lights exploded and speckled the cloudy sky with thousands of beautiful coloured lights. Hundreds of birds were passing by, in full flight from this strange new horror.

Nero would undoubtedly have claimed us as his own as we stood there on the trim lawn beside the idly-dangling magpies, smoking expensive looted cigarettes and happily watching the fireworks – though soon its very immensity appalled us.

The orders for us to continue the retreat arrived while X. Don was still blazing – we were to report to Corps Heavies outside Achiet-le-Grand on the Achiet-le-Petit road. The roads were fairly full, and this time while it would be wrong to say there was a panic the retreat resembled more of a rout than had previously been the case. Everyone seemed anxious to get away as quickly as possible and regardless of anyone else. Cars and lorries found themselves hung up behind such impassable things as pigeon caravans, while slow-moving columns of infantry transport meandered on and off the roads where and when they pleased. A few military policemen dashed up and down on horseback trying to enforce some kind of order, but no one took much notice; had the Germans been able to break through with cavalry or armoured cars the war would have ended for most of us.

Rifle fire sounded very close, and everyone was wondering how many infantry there were between us and the enemy. After about half an hour's struggling our two lorries managed to reach the corner leading into the main Bapaume-Achiet-le-Grand road – we had come about a mile. Here we came to a standstill, and I jumped down to find out the reason. A cyclist on point duty at the corner said to me, "It's no good going on to Achiet along this road, sir, because the bridge is down. You'll have to turn back and go round through Grévillers."

This was a pretty kettle of fish. I knew it would be impossible to attempt even to turn round, let alone work our way back against the traffic on the narrow road to Grévillers – which by this time might have been captured. So, having a faint idea of the geography of Achiet-le-Grand, I told the cyclist that the bridge was on the far side of the village and that we wanted to turn off long before we got to it.

Reluctantly he allowed us to pass, and thanks to his efforts the road in front of us was completely empty. We bowled along merrily at a good ten miles an hour; I looked back and saw that everyone was following us – come what may we had the great advantage of being in front.

But as things turned out I was right and the cyclist was wrong; it was easy to get through Achiet-le-Grand without going anywhere near the bridge because there wasn't one.

I parked our lorries in a side road in the middle of Achiet-le-Grand and walked to the rendezvous to meet the Colonel, who had gone ahead in the car. The rendezvous turned out to be a Divisional headquarters, which struck me as being an odd place for Corps Heavies to tell us to report to.

But a greater surprise was in store. The Colonel met me outside. "Corps Heavies have washed their hands of us," he said. "It has been decided to attach us to 40th Division till things settle down again."

The question of whether Heavy Artillery, like Divisional Field Artillery, should come under the orders of Divisions

[92]

had long been a vexed one, and there were certainly points in favour of it. But at a time of crisis like this it seemed sheer folly. Efficient though a Division may be, you are asking only for trouble to cast at its head at a moment's notice a Heavy Artillery brigade which requires thousands of gallons of petrol for its lorries and tons of ammunition as different from that used by divisional artillery as lead is from feathers.

The Colonel went inside again, and I waited in blank amazement wondering what on earth was going to happen next. I saw Healing our Brigade Major in one of the offices and went to speak to him; he was very fed up at the turn of events. While I was talking to him an inner door opened and two Lieutenant-Generals[1] came out. Both looked very grave as they walked through the room; the Brigade Major whispered that a Corps Commanders' conference had just taken place to decide what was to be done – on our immediate right there was a big gap caused by the rout of Fifth Army, and there was every likelihood of the Germans outflanking us.

In spite of the seriousness of the situation I was able to appreciate its drama; here, passing through this very room, had been the men upon whom depended not only our personal safety but perhaps that of the whole British Expeditionary Force.

The Corps Commanders departed swiftly in their motors, and the Colonel sent me back to guide the lorries to our new destination – 40th Division near Bucquoy. I walked to the lorries; on the way I passed one of the Corps Commanders held up in the traffic like any other mortal.

A big mail from home had somehow just reached us; the Sergeant-major gave me my letters and in one of them I was interested to read, 'Glad to get your note of the 14th. Everyone at home is expecting to hear that the big German offensive has opened, but we are glad you say you don't think they will get very far.'

[1] Probably Fanshawe and Haldane. I would have recognised Harper, the third of the four Corps Commanders of Third Army, because he had previously commanded 51st Division.

Our progress from Achiet-le-Grand to Bucquoy, a distance of about five miles, was a mere crawl. We passed the huts and tents of 40th Division, but there was nowhere where we could turn off and we had to move with the stream.

Half a mile further on we came to a very small side road into which, pursued by the cursing of the traffic which we held up behind us for several minutes, we turned laboriously. The lorries were unloaded in a field by the roadside, and the Colonel and I walked back to Division across the waste of overgrown shell holes.

They seemed extremely busy in the divisional artillery office, and we waited nearly ten minutes before anyone took any notice of us. Then someone introduced the Colonel to the C.R.A.

"You must excuse me," he said to the Colonel. "Things are critical on our sector just now, and my Brigade Major will attend to your wants – there he is."

So the Colonel walked across to the Brigade Major, told him where our batteries were and what size of guns they had, and finished up with, "By the way, we *must* have five hundred gallons of petrol by noon tomorrow at the very latest."

The Brigade Major, taken back, gasped, seized a pencil and jotted down on a scrap of paper '500 gallons of petrol,' and after a short pause said, "Oh ha, right, I'll fix up a scheme."

The Colonel added sourly, "Also we have only enough rations to last us till breakfast tomorrow."

The Brigade Major jotted down 'Rations, 700 men,' and after another short pause said, "Oh ha, right. I'll fix up a scheme."

Then they looked at one another till the utter absurdity of the situation seemed to dawn on them, and they both grinned.

The C.R.A. now joined us and told the Colonel to get his guns limbered up ready to move at a moment's notice and park them on any suitable side road between Achiet-le-Grand and Logeast Wood. "But the situation is changing so fast, you know, that I may have to send you fresh orders at any minute," he concluded. "Leave a runner here so that I can get in touch with you immediately."

The Colonel and I walked back to our field in silence; now that the excitement was over the outlook had never seemed blacker. During a supper of sorts our runner returned with a situation telegram historically interesting enough to warrant inclusion:

> The enemy has occupied Combles, Morval, and Lesboeufs, necessitating a retirement on the right of Third Army AAA As soon as it is dark tonight 40th Division will leave outposts on its present front line and withdraw to the following approximate line AAA H 9 central, B 27 central, B 21 central, B 9 d 6.2, where they will join with 31st Division AAA 42nd Division as soon as it can get up will take over the above line relieving 40th Division whose outposts will then retire through the line AAA As soon as the infantry relief is complete the G.O.C. 42nd Division will take over command of the sector from the G.O.C. 40th Division, when the divisional sector will pass from the command of VI Corps to IV Corps AAA 40th Div. Arty. will be relieved by 42nd Div. Arty. night 25th-26th AAA On relief 40th Div. Arty. will march direct to Douchy-les-Ayette.
>
> From 40th Div. Arty. 7.45 PM, March 24.

This telegram did not really affect our movements; it merely notified us that we were to be bandied from 40th to 42nd Division – the Division with which I spent the first year of the war, and which, as fate would have it, remained with IV Corps and shared its successes from that day till the armistice, when I last saw them marching blithely towards Charleroi.

The Colonel and I went off in the car to give our batteries the news and to choose a suitable side road. On the way we picked up Aglionby and the Majors of Toc 1 and Toc 4. It was a fine moonlit night and the roads along which we drove were empty. Thompson must have taken us nearly into Bapaume. We could see the flashes of batteries on all sides, but whether they were British or German we neither knew nor cared. Nothing seemed to matter, for such was the reaction after the strains and stresses of the past three days. Once, coming to a dead end, we turned round and drove back the way we had come; in the middle of the road yawned a large shell hole which had not been there five minutes earlier. The Vauxhall took it in its stride. Once a field battery opened fire from behind the hedge alongside the road and all but blew us out of the car. I fell asleep and woke up to find that the road for parking the hows. had already been chosen and that we were on the way back to our head-quarters.

The congestion, bad enough in the afternoon, was now so much worse that nothing was moving. The Colonel jumped out of the car and walked on ahead, cursing right and left. The chief cause of the trouble was a heavy battery which had tried to bank round a field battery. The result was a deadlock, and the drivers, far from trying to straighten things out, were asleep in their saddles. They soon woke up, how-ever, when the Colonel addressed them, and after much shouting and swearing they made a lane through which Thompson was just able to drive. For the next mile the traffic was stationary, but the car was so narrow that we were able to creep along in low gear. Nearly everybody was asleep; no one seemed to care in the least how long he stayed there. The Colonel became more and more furious and vented the full force of his wrath on a cringing lorry driver who had fallen asleep at his wheel, thereby leaving a gap of several hundred yards between his lorry and the one next in front.

We reached our field and turned in thankfully in an old tent which the excellent Sergeant-major had found, but I was hardly asleep when a runner arrived from Division with fresh orders. The situation had changed materially; our batteries were to continue the retreat at dawn and put Logeast Wood between them and the enemy.

The Colonel and Thompson and I were the only ones at brigade who knew where the batteries were to be found; the orders were too urgent to entrust to either of the dispatch-riders who, reliable though they always were, might take

Toc 1 loading a 9·2-in. howitzer. Note the size, and therefore the weight, of a 9·2 shell. The cordite cartridges can be seen
in a pile on the right

Toc 3 in action near Logeast Wood on March 25
(6-in. howitzer)

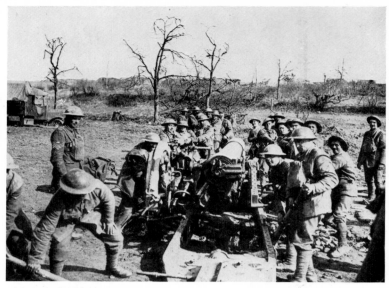

Toc 4 pulling out on March 23 after having fired 200 rounds
into Mory (6-in. howitzer)

Toc 5 on the move near Bapaume during the retreat
(6-in. Mark XIX gun)

hours to find everyone. So I volunteered to go the rounds on one of their motor-cycles.

The Colonel agreed; he seemed pretty well exhausted. But what with the new excitement and the sleep in the car I felt perfectly fresh.

I set off. The traffic on the main road was still at a stand-still; the only difference I noticed was that the gap between the two lorries had closed up. It was a difficult ride. The Triumph was not going well and its clutch was out of action; time and again I bumped against horses or scraped my knuckles on the side of some wagon or lorry I was trying to pass. In the middle of Achiet-le-Grand the engine gave up the ghost; after wasting five precious minutes trying to entice it back I shoved the bike into the ditch and left it.

My luck was in. At the far end of the village I passed a shed beneath which stood half a dozen beautiful gleaming Triumphs. I crept up to them – joy, no one was about – and chose the newest-looking one. Pulling it off its stand, I pushed it silently into the road, turned on the petrol, tickled the carburetter, and vigorously kicked the starter. It wouldn't start. At that very moment a man came out of the house and walked past the shed into the road. Panic struck me and I was just about to leave the bike and run away when a better idea came into my head. The man was walking past without paying much attention to me; I saw on his arm a couple of stripes and the blue and white badge of Signals – he must be a dispatch-rider, possibly even the owner of the bicycle I was borrowing. . . . Never mind, chance it.

"Corporal!" I called sternly. "Please help me to start my bike. She's a bit cold, I think."

He came to my side, injected a squirt of petrol into the cylinder – of course, how stupid of me! – and jumped on the kick-starter. The engine started immediately with a roar.

"Thanks awfully!" I shouted, getting astride.

"You're welcome, sir," he shouted back, when he must have realized.

"Hi *YOU*!" he yelled. "That's *my* bike!"

But he was too late.

I found the officers of Toc 1 and Toc 4 sleeping in their valises beside their hows. In valises all men look alike, and since I had no torch I made a few unpopular mistakes by rousing the wrong sleepers.

I rode on, stopping briefly at Toc 3 on the way, and found Toc 2, always with an eye to the main chance, in occupation of a row of comfortable huts on the eastern outskirts of Logeast Wood. Their officers were still up and enjoying a merry evening on Bapaume Canteen, and once more I joined them for a spell. Then, utterly worn out, I made my way back to the tent. I reached it at 3 AM, and by one minute past I was fast asleep.

CHAPTER XI

March 25

I woke up a few hours later cold, damp, stiff. The cooks had left the firewood out in the rain and there was not a drop of petrol to spare for the fire; there would be no tea for hours and hours. Had life ever been more unbearable, I wondered, listening to the rain pattering down on the tent.

The morning wore on very slowly. The batteries had moved at dawn and were now in action in various positions on the westerly end of the road through Logeast Wood – which, by the way, was a wood only in name. It was impossible to lay lines to them; we had hardly any wire left.

At eleven o'clock a situation report arrived from Division; our front line was practically the same as that described in the situation report of the previous evening except that we had lost about a thousand yards on the northern part of the divisional sector. Bapaume was now well inside the German lines. The telegram ended with that irritating platitude:

> Keep well clear of above line. Short shooting has been constant.

An hour later, however, a note arrived by runner from Aglionby:

> Infantry brigadier here reports he is not holding Sapignies and Béhagnies and has asked me to fire on them.

Gilly, who had been tearing here, there, and everywhere on his motor-cycle in search of petrol, happened to be with us when Aglionby's note arrived. "By Jove," he said thoughtfully, "there's a billiard table in the Club at Béhagnies. I do hope they've been able to get it away."[1]

[1] They had.

In the end a lorry filled with petrol tins arrived from Siege Park. The big difficulty proved to be distribution, because the congestion on the roads was nearly as bad as on the previous day.

We were still drawing ammunition from Puisieux, but a lorry can carry only fifty rounds of 6-inch how. ammunition at a time and it took anything up to six hours for it to work its way from the batteries to the dump and back again, and even then it was lucky if it got through. Indeed our hundred lorries were by now hopelessly lost, stolen, or strayed; at last the Colonel in despair stood at the corner by the main road and tried to buttonhole every passing empty lorry, regardless of the unit to which it belonged. On this occasion and though fluent and persuasive he met with scant success; at the end of an hour he had secured one for certain plus two doubtful ones who said they would turn round at the next corner and come back.

In the early afternoon orders arrived that the brigade was to continue the retreat at once and report to Corps Heavies again at Acheux Château, a jump of some ten miles. The experiment of attaching us to a Division had not lasted long.

The Colonel and Gardiner went off in the car to get the orders through to the batteries; I was left behind with a motor-cycle to superintend the departure of our own two lorries, after which I was to wait "as long as possible" (in case any of our batteries should miss the Colonel and come to brigade for orders) and then ride on to Acheux to meet the Colonel.

I pushed off our lorries within a quarter of an hour and sat down on the roadbank, feeling very small and lonely.

The traffic was now moving with a swing, and after I had waited half an hour big gaps began to appear and occasional field batteries went past at the trot. How long was 'as long as possible,' I began to wonder anxiously, and I started up the motor-cycle to make sure it would go all right when the time came.

The traffic was getting less and less; at last I noticed that people were apprehensively looking behind them as though expecting the Germans. Five minutes later I could stick it no longer, and I got on the motor-cycle and rode into Bucquoy.

Events were exciting indeed. Military policemen with drawn revolvers were directing the traffic, which was now moving at a gallop. Horse transport was being sent by one road, motor transport by another. A smart, clean-looking battalion of infantry had just arrived; the soldiers were filing into the houses and gardens at the eastern end of the village. Machine-gunners were testing their machine-guns, and Lewis-gunners were making loopholes in the walls. It was obvious that the enemy was not far away.

I felt I ought to hang on a minute or two longer, and I waited beside the military policemen. Then I saw the most welcome sight of all – the brigade car. Thompson was driving furiously, and the Colonel, wearing his tin hat for once, yelled as he swept past, "They've all got away. Come on!"

I afterwards heard that Thompson had distinguished himself by taking the wrong turning, thereby driving the car through a hot German barrage. The road was blocked, and he had to turn round and drive back through the same barrage.

I followed the car, and I had not gone very far before I heard the crackle of musketry behind me. The Germans had reached Bucquoy.

For the next couple of miles we all moved along at twenty miles an hour, but when we had passed through Puisieux the pace slowed down considerably. Half a mile further on I caught up the brigade lorries; seeing one of the dispatch-riders sitting on the tail-board, I shouted to him to hop off and take over the motor-cycle, and I climbed up on the front seat beside Fulton and promptly dozed off.

I woke several times during the journey. Once I heard someone shout, "Halt! Action left!" to a field battery which swung off the road immediately in front of us, and I saw one battalion of infantry bivouacking in the open, another clearing out an overgrown trench – disused since 1916 – with their entrenching tools. I also remember passing a notice which announced THIS IS SERRE, and only those who have seen can visualize the utterness of the desolation.

Our entry into Mailly-Maillet gave me pleasure because it contained the first complete houses I had seen for weeks. Wondering women and children stood at the doors and gates of their cottages and watched us driving past; they did not seem to grasp what had happened.

The scenery looked so different and was changing so quickly that we seemed to be in another world; it was more like going on leave than fleeing from the Germans. There were windmills at Colincamps and at Bertrancourt, and whenever I see a windmill now I think of dust and lorries and flight.

We rattled through Bertrancourt; last time we had been there we were on our way to Gézaincourt for our fortnight's rest. Next, between Bertrancourt and Acheux, we passed the railhead which, though we would not have believed it then, was to be our future ammunition dump. Not far from it stood the tall factory chimney which the Colonel – and no one else – afterwards wished to use as a reserve O.P.

At last we pulled up beside the Y.M.C.A. in the square of Acheux; it seemed the Y.M.C.A. were giving their stock away. Our men rushed in for tea and biscuits, but after the sack of Bapaume Canteen mere giving away seemed flat. The shops round the square were anxiously selling off at bargain prices.

Five minutes later the brigade car arrived and we followed it into the château grounds, scattering right and left fat ducks and angry geese. The Colonel hurried into the château to report to General Marshall. Half an hour later we were off again, but only, thank goodness, to park our lorries and hows. on the Acheux-Forceville road and billet in Forceville for the night.

The Colonel stood in the middle of Forceville directing the traffic like a military policeman; as soon as our hows., Four-Wheel Drives, and lorries were all neatly parked in line along the road he sent me back to the château to report that all our batteries had arrived safely except Toc 1, which was missing. Nothing was known of them, except that they had been very short of petrol.

General Marshall and Major Healing were sitting in a large and beautifully furnished *salon*. I told them the news and was turning to go when an orderly entered. As I was closing the door the General shouted, "Come back!"

"How long will it take you to get to Colonel Thorp?" he asked.

"About four minutes, sir."

"Then get off as quickly as you can and tell him to continue to retreat *at once*. The Germans captured Albert half an hour ago. Make for Doullens. Either the Brigade Major or I will be at the Town Hall there to give you fresh orders. Hurry up – Forceville is only six miles from Albert."

I ran to my motor-cycle. Heavens, Doullens was another twelve miles on – some retreat, this, would it ever stop? I tore so fast along the Acheux-Forceville road that people rushed out of the way and turned to stare.

The Colonel was still standing complacently in the middle of Forceville, surveying the neatly stretched-out brigade with a proud and fatherly eye. The lorry drivers were wiping down their lorries, the gunners were cleaning their guns. Billets had already been chosen for half the brigade; the other half had found its way into the estaminets.

Within twelve minutes we were all on the move again, and with real dismay in our hearts. It was growing dark. Dust and petrol vapour was everywhere, filling ears and eyes, nose and mouth. The great trees which flanked the broad straight road loomed up and faded away in endless succession. The roar of the lorry became a lullaby, and I fell into an uneasy doze. Once we stopped, and I woke to be told some big gun in front of us had fallen off the road. Our lorries could only just squeeze past. Half awake, I saw kilometre stone after kilometre stone go by till it seemed like a game in which distance, villages, and woods all meant nothing; I found it difficult to convince myself that we were still in flight. Yet in the days which followed I journeyed many dozen times along the Doullens-Acheux road, and never again did it seem so interminable.

We passed through Louvencourt and Vauchelles, Marieux and Sarton; between Sarton and Orville a dispatch-rider overtook us.

"Nine-O Brigade?" he shouted.

"Yes, that's us."

"I've a letter from Corps Heavies."

The Colonel read it. We were to park for the night in Orville, where the men were to be billeted, and at nine in the morning the Colonel was to report for orders at the Town Hall, Doullens.

We soon found billets for most of the men. The car was driven off the road into a field, and the Colonel lighted his primus stove and cooked our supper – twopenny soup-squares and champagne.

After supper the Colonel and Gardiner prepared to spend the night in the car, but Gilly, Benwell, and I partially unloaded a lorry, swept it out, and unrolled our valises on its floor. While we were undressing the Colonel strolled over.

"Call yourselves soldiers?" he asked contemptuously. "I want two of you to be up at six and push off on motor-cycles to see if you can find Toc 1. One of you search the roads the way we came; the other towards Authie and Souastre. And don't get captured."

Quarrelling among ourselves about which of us should not get up at six, we turned in.

CHAPTER XII

March 26 & 27

"Come on, come on!" the Colonel was shouting angrily, and Gilly, Benwell, and I woke up. Glory be – it was seven o'clock!

"Get up at once," he said, lifting the back curtain of the lorry. "Gardiner's been off for nearly an hour."

Feeling ashamed of ourselves, we quickly put on our clothes and pushed off. It was a lovely spring morning, the birds were singing, the sun was just melting the mist. Everything seemed fresh and sweet and clean. My motor-cycle – still the one I had stolen – was going perfectly; a faint trail of pale blue smoke from its exhaust hung lazily a few inches above the road. No joy ride has been more delightful.

I met Gardiner in Marieux.

"No use going this way!" he shouted. "I've been nearly as far as Colincamps – the Boche is there. No sign of Toc 1 anywhere."

During the next half-hour Gilly and Benwell returned. Neither of them had any news; the roads, they said, were pretty well empty for at least ten miles.

We all began to fear the worst, but just as the Colonel was starting off for Doullens Toc 3's Ford came bumping down the road – and in it was the Major of Toc 1.

"Where's your battery?" the Colonel shouted.

"Coming into Orville now along the Pas road, sir."

It was the one road we had not searched.

Major Pargiter looked more fed up than I had seen him before; his uniform, face, and tin hat were so covered with dust that he looked like a miller. "I had to abandon one how., sir," he said stiffly. "One of my Four-Wheel Drives ran out of petrol. I couldn't get any more and we've been marching all night."

Bit by bit his story unfolded – how the congestion the previous afternoon had been so great that all roads to Puisieux were blocked and he had been forced to turn north towards Fonquevillers with the intention of making for Doullens, where he expected to be able to find out our whereabouts. He had made his men march so as to economize petrol and had emptied his last tins into the Four-Wheel Drives, but one of them had run dry at Ayette. After trying in vain to make another Four-Wheel Drive pull two hows., they had finally abandoned it. They reached Pas to find the village in an extraordinary panic. VI Corps headquarters were feverishly packing up, and barricades were being erected across the streets to stop the Boche armoured cars, said to be tearing towards them down the Arras road at thirty miles an hour – our front line at Arras had hardly shifted a yard, by the way – and he and his weary gunners were actually ordered to line the heights outside the village with their rifles. And, most scandalous of all, staff officers had commandeered one of their precious ammunition lorries to move their personal kit.

The Colonel could contain his anger no longer. "Low swine," he growled, and departed, no doubt to tell Corps Heavies all about it. But to the rest of us nothing mattered now that Toc 1 had turned up and the brigade was still intact.

The Colonel returned with more orders from Corps Heavies: the whole brigade was to move at once to Mézerolles, a village five miles west of Doullens, to rest for a couple of days and at the same time do its utmost to refit ready to enter the battle again. Ordnance had already been ordered to give us top priority, and indents for important deficiencies were to be submitted at once.

So we set off on what proved to be the last stage of the Great Retreat. The road was full of refugees, and a Company of 'Chinks' – Chinese Labour Corps – was on the march too – at least they were straggling from Orville almost into

Doullens, and provided welcome comic relief. They were behaving more like school children unexpectedly let out of school; they grinned at everyone and everything, and trickled in twos and threes into every estaminet they passed. Some were carrying great bundles of kit on their heads, others seemed to possess nothing more than the flimsy clothes they were wearing. Some were helping refugees to wheel the barrow or handcart in which lay their pathetic household goods, others ran happily after our lorries hoping vainly for a lift.

We stopped for a minute or two on the outskirts of Doullens, and I saw two Chinese enter a lingerie shop. They were ejected at once, and they stood on the pavement chattering and gesticulating like angry monkeys.

There was great activity round the Town Hall. Judging by the number of magnificent cars standing outside there were important people within, and I thought I saw the Commander-in-Chief's car with its miniature Union Jack. Big French cars were waiting too. We did not know that Marshal Foch was there, and it was only recently that I came across the following:

Le Matin publishes an extract from a new book by its editor, M. Stedhane Lauzanne, in which he traces in all its details the historical scene at Doullens, when on March 26 1918 Marshal Foch was appointed Commander-in-Chief of all the armies. He writes:

M. Clemenceau on Sunday March 23, the third day of the German offensive on the Somme and the Oise, went to find M. Poincaré to tell him that owing to the situation it would perhaps be prudent to evacuate Paris. M. Poincaré objected. M. Clemenceau returned the same evening to Compiègne and telephoned M. Poincaré that General Pétain was of the same opinion as was M. Clemenceau himself.

M. Poincaré the same night wrote M. Clemenceau to explain his objections, and asked him to call a meeting of Ministers. This was held next day, but M. Clemenceau had already somewhat changed his opinion and announced to the Ministers that on March 26 an interview would be held at

Doullens with a representative of the British Government, and proposed that the President of the Republic should accompany him.

On March 26 M. Poincaré accordingly went to Doullens and was informed that Sir Douglas Haig was in conference with his Army Commanders and that it would be better not to disturb him. Accompanying M. Poincaré were MM. Clemenceau and Loucheur, also Marshal Foch who, in the course of conversation with M. Poincaré, informed him that serious orders had just been issued comprising an almost general retreat of the Army and involving very soon the evacuation of Paris.

These orders seemed to produce extreme excitement in Marshal Foch, who kept on repeating, 'The Boches! Why, they can always be stopped! It is sufficient only to give the order.'

'But how do you stop them?' M. Loucheur inquired.

'You know my plan,' replied Foch. 'I simply place a stickfast here and another there, and the Boches can go no further.'

The English conference being ended, the Anglo-French conference now began. M. Poincaré spoke first. He explained the situation, and added that for him there was no question of stopping the Boches anywhere except where they were then, and not elsewhere. Sir Douglas Haig spoke next, and said that for his part he was prepared to do his best and defend Amiens.

Marshal Foch sprang forward and cried, 'No! It is not a question of Amiens. We must first conquer where we are now!' In a few words he went on to urge that the Boches must be stopped at once, and for this it was sufficient to give the order.

At this moment Lord Milner rose and signed to M. Clemenceau, to whom he repeatedly said, 'This is the man!' Sir Douglas Haig also rose and joined Lord Milner and M. Clemenceau.

Sir Douglas energetically pleaded in favour of a single command. 'We have our only remedy,' he said, 'and that is to put over me and over Pétain a chief to whom we will both be responsible. As for me, I would willingly place myself under the orders of Foch. I had already telegraphed this to my Government 48 hours ago.'

M. Clemenceau returned to the table and in a loud voice proposed to General Pétain to do the same as Sir Douglas Haig and place himself under the orders of Foch.

The declaration was then drawn up appointing Foch Commander-in-Chief.

We moved on through Doullens; whom should we pass on the road but Toc 5, ordered to leave us at Grévillers. Three miles ahead at the Mézerolles road corner we halted for twenty minutes to await the return of the officers who had gone on ahead to arrange billets. There was an estaminet on the corner, and I ate a meal the like of which I had not expected to taste again – coffee mixed with rum and a large omelette.

We then turned down the hill into Mézerolles, a delectable village lying a quarter of a mile to the left of the main road and well below it. It straggled, but not unpleasantly like the villages of Artois. It possessed all the qualifications of a village in Arcady – a rambling stream, an old stone bridge, a quaint little church, a twisting main street, a gay Mairie, a well-stocked estaminet, and at its far end it ran into a wooded hill and suddenly stopped, as though surprised at its audacity.

We billeted ourselves in the end farm just below the hill. Gardiner ran out lines to the houses where the batteries had billeted themselves, and for the next two days the wires buzzed not with such messages as 'S.O.S. Left Division' or 'Fire 30 rounds at Bapaume station' but 'How many great-coats are you deficient of?' or 'Reply at once to my signal re number of lorries out of action.'

Toc 2 – of course – established a firm liaison with the R.F.C. Squadron occupying a temporary landing ground nearby; its pilots listened enviously to tales of Bapaume Canteen, and many a box of cigars was bartered for flips over the line.

We slept, cleaned ourselves, and examined our wounds. We had lost only one how. out of twenty-two – the one which Toc 2 had ditched in the shell hole at Maricourt Wood on March 21. The how. abandoned by Toc 1 at Ayette on March 25 had been found and salved by one of the horse-drawn batteries of our old friends 48 Brigade R.G.A. In addition Toc 1 had lost a 9·2 barrel which had toppled into the Ancre while crossing Miraumont Bridge. Macartney, the A.S.C. subaltern who went to the rescue, had an anxious and stirring time while trying to recover it, and his account of how the accident happened and of the energetic steps he took when he heard of it will be found on page 164. When we advanced five months later Major Pargiter made a bee-line for Miraumont Bridge, but the barrel had gone – perhaps to adorn the Tiergarten in Berlin.

Our casualties had been light considering the severity of the fighting – 12 killed, 43 wounded, and a few missing, figures which do not include the casualties inflicted by the 9·45 shell which had burst among the reinforcements at Grévillers. Our losses in gun stores and kit were great, but the firm which employed us was a big one and soon able to make them good – though the magic words 'Lost in the retreat' served so frequently that at last a G.R.O. – General Routine Order – was published forbidding their use.

On the morning of the second day at Mézerolles Major Pargiter came round to complain strongly about being out of the battle, and he asked for permission to go off on a roving commission with one Four-Wheel Drive carrying thirty rounds of ammunition and towing one 6-inch how. The Colonel listened sympathetically, but after consultation with Corps Heavies he had to refuse; it had been laid down by Army that infantry and field artillery were to have sole use of the roads at present.

The same afternoon a car went along the Doullens road, where Major Clark of Toc 4 happened to be inspecting his hows., and a staff officer leant out and asked hysterically, "What are all these guns doing back here? They ought to be in the line!"

We wondered if he was one of the staff officers who had taken Toc 1's ammunition lorry.

That evening orders arrived that on the following morning the brigade was to reconnoitre for battery positions in the Bertrancourt area and to hold itself in readiness to move into action at an hour's notice. Though remaining under the command of Corps Heavies we were to work with and for the New Zealand Division, now arriving in Doullens from reserve in the back areas.

CHAPTER XIII

March 28 & 29

Early next morning the Colonel and the four battery commanders and I drove back towards the line. Doullens was packed; the New Zealand Division was detraining at the station. Doullens itself was recovering fast, and already shops were reopening and prices soaring; it was said that a French division would arrive shortly too.

The Doullens-Acheux road was almost empty, and things seemed to be settling down splendidly. Marieux Château, the lovely home of IV Corps Headquarters, was a centre of reassuring activity. From Authie to Bus-les-Artois we drove through budding woods. Battalions of big New Zealanders resting by the roadside cursed us loudly as we spattered them with mud. Chinese were hard at work digging reserve lines – which were not used.

Bus was full. Interpreters attached to the New Zealand Division were hurrying about with notebooks in their hands searching volubly for billets for Divisional Trench Mortars, for the Divisional Supply Company, for the A.P.M., the C.R.E., Ordnance, and a dozen more. Officers were seeking sites for the Salvage Dump, for the Divisional Canteen, and for the Prisoner-of-War cage. The Château had just been taken over for Divisional Headquarters; it would not be easy to find a billet anywhere in Bus, and we drove on. At the Colincamps corner stood a New Zealand military policeman as smart as if there wasn't a German within fifty miles.

"No," he said, "you can't go along the Colincamps road. The diggers have only just driven the Boche out and they're working forward to Mailly-Maillet now."

So we went to Bertrancourt instead, where the Colonel left me to find a billet for brigade headquarters and pushed on towards Beaussart with the others to look for battery positions. But Bertrancourt was hopelessly full of infantry and Maori pioneers and wagon lines, and I walked back through the mud to Bus and told the first interpreter I saw that we were the Heavy Artillery now attached to his Division and that we therefore *must* find a headquarters somewhere in Bus.

"No," he said. "Sorry. Eet is impossible, full up."

"But your Divisional Commander will be angry when he learns that the Heavy Artillery attached to his Division is unable to find a billet."

"Perhaps I will see what can be done. Let us try Billet No. 32."

But Billet No. 32 was too small and too dirty.

"No," I said firmly, "I cannot ask the commander of a Heavy Artillery Brigade to live in such a house."

"Is eet for the commander of a Heavy Artillery Brigade himself that you seek a billet?"

"Yes."

"Then I think Billet No. 91 will suit your General admirably. Would you care for me to lead you there?"

Off we went together to Billet No. 91, a low and charming red-roofed house with a big garden in front, and there I made the acquaintance of Monsieur, a nice old schoolmaster, of Mathilde his shrewish wife, and of Jeanette their graceful and pretty daughter.

"Yes," I told the interpreter, "this will suit us perfectly, and the General will be very pleased. I should like that big room for his bedroom, and, if it would not inconvenience Madame, that small room beside it for the office and mess. And also the cellar for the telephone exchange."

"No, no!" protested Madame. "The cellar is impossible – the cider and the potatoes!"

"*Ça ne fait rien, Mathilde,*" interposed Monsieur gently.

But Madame was adamant – until the interpreter had spoken rapidly to her for several minutes about *La France* and *réquisitions* and such like. Monsieur stood silent and nodded approvingly, while Jeanette winked at me and smiled and pouted and danced on her toes.

H   [113]

Then we all sealed the bargain with a bottle of Graves, and I walked back through the mud to Bertrancourt to meet the Colonel. We drove back to Mézerolles where we loaded our lorries, and next morning the whole brigade moved back to the war, to the excitement of crowds of waving children and tearful old women.

In Doullens the King drove past us.

CHAPTER XIV

Army Book 136

The great March offensive burned itself out like a forest fire, but there was no anticlimax for us during the weeks and months which followed. Optimism did not come till August, anticipation of final victory even later – and, when it did come, almost with a rush. But from April onwards, at any rate on our sector of the front, one was conscious of a prevailing spirit of profound thankfulness, almost of satisfaction, that the Germans were securely held. Of the two factors which contributed most to this happy feeling, the first was the daily evidence around us that now it was ourselves and not the Germans who were living and fighting in a green and wooded countryside hardly touched by the spoiling hand of war. The second and greater factor was our rapidly growing friendship with the New Zealand Division, with whom we now were working as closely as if we had been their own Divisional field artillery brigade.

We admired them more than any Division we had previously met, and not only because we knew them better. They accepted us too, and in a matter of days they looked upon us as their private heavy artillery. Except when they were out of the line we were in daily contact with them till the end of the war – and with battalions and even companies as well as with their Divisional and Brigade headquarters. I cannot recall a single occasion when either side let the other down. For us, bearing in mind that Heavy Artillery Brigades were Corps troops, it was a novel and stimulating experience, and I have no doubt we shot all the better for it. For no words of mine can convey to the layman the feeling of heaven which an artilleryman knows when the Division he is supporting is a good one, and of all the good

[115]

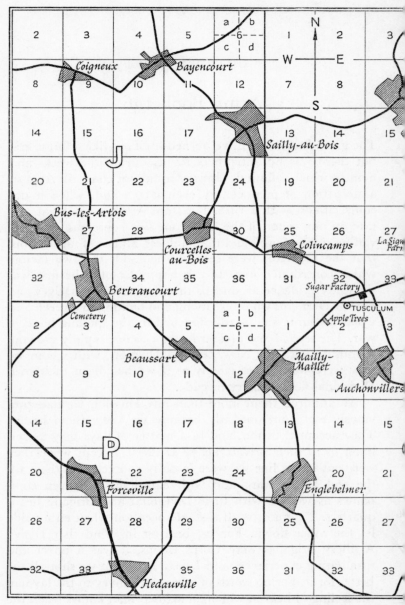

The Brigade's battle-front,

	Gommecourt	a	b		Bucquoy				
4	5	--6--		1	2		4	5
		c	d					
10	11	12	7	8	9	10	11
Hébuterne							
16	17	18	13	14	15	16	17
		Louverval Farm					
				Puisieux-au-Mont		L	
22	23	24	19	20	21	22	23
	John Copse						
	Luke Copse Mark Copse						
28	Matthew Copse 29		25	26	27	28	29
		Serre				Beauregard Dovecote	
		Pendant Copse					
34	35	36	31	32	33	34	35
						Miraumont	
4	5	a b --6-- c d	1	2	3	4	5
		Beaumont-Hamel					
10	11	12		8		10	11
		Beaucourt-sur-Ancre			Grandcourt		
16	17	18	13	14	15	16	17
						R	
22	23	24	19	20	21	22	23
							Courcelette
Mesnil	29	30		26	27	28	29
				Thiepval			
34	35	36	31	32	33	34	35
		Authuille					

March 30 – August 21

For scale etc., see note
under map on page 54

and very good Divisions of the British army I would rate the New Zealand Division high among the highest.

Yet, well though we ourselves were placed, many were not so fortunate. The Germans still had several heavy shots left in their locker. In early April they launched a powerful surprise attack on the Lys – from our point of view luckily forty miles to our north. The Portuguese took the brunt of the initial onslaught and broke; the 55th (West Lancashire) Division, mostly of Liverpool men, came in and saved the situation by their endurance and courage. In another savage offensive at the end of April the Germans swept over Kemmel Hill and Messines Ridge; they failed to capture Ypres too. At the same time they struck hard at Amiens, but the Australians fought them to a standstill at Villers Bretonneux fifteen miles to our south.

I can best refresh my memory about our own doings in April and for three more months to come by glancing through the pages of our daily log, kept in a succession of ruled Crown-sized notebooks unromantically entitled Army Book 136. Each lasted us about a couple of months, and in each was entered – day and night, oddly enough invariably in pencil, by whichever officer of headquarters happened to be on duty – every fighting order or message we sent out or received. It was thus kept by Gardiner, Benwell[1] and myself, and in the daytime the Colonel often took a turn too.

I still possess the log which covered the period from March 30 to June 9. Its first entry, timed 11.31 AM, is in my writing – neater than usual as befits the first entry in a new book – and reports a Germany battery at K 18 c 9.5 (*close beside the track past Louverval Farm*) now firing. I see I instructed Toc 2 to shoot 10 rounds at it, and, since this figure is enclosed in a square thus 10, they did so.

---

[1] It must be by reason of his self-effacement that I have said so little of Benwell, our Orderly Officer, a quiet, reliable, and trustworthy man of much the same age as Gardiner and myself. He came, I seem to remember, from Birmingham; he was a thinker and a doer rather than a talker, and he was always there when needed.

The second entry, in the Colonel's writing and timed 2.0 PM, ordered Toc 5 – once more restored to our fatherly care – to fire 30 rounds at R 9 a 1.5 (*north bank of Ancre from Grandcourt*), where our New Zealand liaison officer reported Germans massing. A long-range target, it will be noted from the map, 12,000 yards – seven miles – from their guns.

At 2.5 PM, again in the Colonel's writing, Toc 1, Toc 2, Toc 3, and Toc 4 were all ordered to put down quite a heavy barrage of 1 round per gun per minute, reducing after 10 minutes to 1 round per gun per 4 minutes, on German trenches and back areas between Serre and Beaumont Hamel, this at the request of Left Brigade of New Zealand Division. On that task the four batteries fired 72, 66, 68, and 92 rounds respectively: I cannot say why Toc 4 fired many more rounds than the other batteries and no doubt the Colonel asked them to explain. In the meantime Toc 5 had fired only 16 of the 30 rounds ordered, and gave the not very satisfactory reason that their guns were suffering from excessive recoil.

At 4.40 PM I see I ordered Toc 4 to fire 1 round per battery per 3 minutes – mere harassing fire, this – at a stretch of road between Serre and Mailly-Maillet, keeping it up for two hours, and the day, an easy one, ended with Corps Heavies sending us the night's S.O.S. lines – roads, tracks, and trenches in the neighbourhood of Beaumont Hamel and Beaucourt – which we duly parcelled out to the batteries, adding the instruction that if they were required to shoot the rate of fire was to be 1 round per gun per 2 minutes for 10 minutes, and then cease fire.

Before turning over the pages of the log and picking out a few of its more interesting or entertaining entries I feel I should speak as a gunner and say a little about general trends and their influence upon the brigade's activities.

In the earlier weeks after the retreat the front line, if I may use a homely metaphor of jam-making, had not quite set; it was apparent that here and there the Germans, still hoping to advance further, were probing and testing. Hence

in April our shoots were mainly in support of the New
Zealand infantry brigades – for example trenches, massing
Germans, roads or road junctions which they were seen or
known to use, machine-gun nests, even active German field
guns. Targets came to us from many sources, including the
brigade O.P.[1] But as April passed and May arrived we were
decreasingly employed in this way, and we resumed our true
role – the neutralization of the enemy's heavy artillery.

When the retreat ended our 6-inch batteries chose excellent positions at Bertrancourt, Beaussart, and Mailly-Maillet.
Toc 5 went in behind Bertrancourt cemetery, and brigade
headquarters moved forward too. Toc 1 initially returned
into action in the midst of Beaussart railway sidings, and
Major Pargiter, spending a morning at the O.P., looked
round and saw a column of smoke rising from them. "Tell
that infernal engine to move on at once before it gives the
battery position away," he ordered on the telephone. "It's
not an engine, sir," the battery command post replied, "it's
the shed where all the officers' kit was." From Beaussart
sidings Toc 1 shortly moved to Bayencourt; by one of war's
little ironies it was the village where their first battery
position had been when they arrived from England nearly
two years before.

The new front line is shown on the map and did not alter
appreciably till August. Brigade targets were mostly but not
entirely within the quadrilateral bounded by Puisieux,
Miramont, Thiepval, and Serre – an area of ghosts, total
obliteration, and of place-names alive and notorious to this
day in the minds of many who survived the Battle of the
Somme.

During the afternoon and early evening of April 6 there
was a flap, and since it was typical of many flaps – in its
confusion and uncertainty too – I describe it from start
to finish as seen through the eyes of brigade headquarters.

[1] Named Tusculum after the old one, it was sited on a hill a short
distance from the scant remains of the sugar factory on the Mailly-Mallet-
Serre road, and within a thousand yards of the front line.

It began at 5.50 PM when the F.O.O. at Tusculum reported exceptionally heavy shelling of the road near the ruined sugar factory, therefore near him too, and he added that red and green rockets, also red and white ones, were going up from the front line on a grid bearing of 30°, that is in the direction of La Signy Farm. At 6.15, on orders from Corps Heavies, we told Toc 2 and Toc 3 to fire 'Concentration C' (10 *rounds each at the Puisieux road north of Beaucourt*), and at 6.30 PM Toc 2, Toc 3, and Toc 4 were warned to stand by in readiness to fire into the area behind La Signy Farm. At 6.40 the stand-by was cancelled, but at 7.1 there was an S.O.S. on the front of V Corps (*the Corps on our right*). Though of no immediate concern to IV Corps, we ordered Toc 2, Toc 3, and Toc 4 to respond by firing 3 rounds per gun at John Copse in front of Puisieux. This was quickly followed by orders to Toc 2 and Toc 3 to fire Concentration C again. Simultaneously Tusculum reported that the road by the sugar factory was once more being heavily shelled, and at 7.27 we sent an S.O.S. stand-by warning – on our own Corps front this time – to Toc 2, Toc 3, and Toc 4, who at 7.40 were all ordered to fire 1 round per gun per 5 minutes on their S.O.S. lines. At 8.0 PM they were told to continue till 8.15, but the flap was nearly over and at 8.1 they were sent the message 'Normal Conditions.'

April 12   At lunch time there were two minor affairs, both of which went according to the drill book. The Brigade Major of the Right Brigade of New Zealand Division telephoned to report a battery Now Firing from Thiepval; with the consent of Corps Heavies Toc 3 engaged it. Initial corrections of '200 yards short' and '100 yards left' were received verbally from a New Zealand observer in an O.P. on the outskirts of Auchonvillers, and before many minutes he reported the enemy battery silenced. No sooner was this over than we received, from the air, a FAN LL [*Infantry, Fleeting Opportunity*] call. From the pin-points given the target was moving on a road near Serre, and Toc 2 and Toc 4 both engaged, firing 20 rounds each.

April 16   At 6.25 PM Toc 4 had a satisfying and not very usual experience when their F.O.O. saw from Apple Trees, a hardly-recognizable orchard close to Tusculum, a German battery in action near Pendant Copse, a distance from him of 5000 yards. He reported it and his battery engaged it. He conducted the shoot visually, and the German battery was silenced after 30 rounds had been fired at it.

April 21   At 3 PM Toc 5 engaged a German balloon on the ground at Dyke Road near Le Sars, and fired 20 rounds at it at a range of 15,000 yards. They reported, 'Splendid results, balloon chased.' I must add that Major Austin, the battery commander, was an endearing man if an unsoldierly type, and the claims of his battery were often a source of amusement to us.

April 22   'Neutralize LY 5 [*the code name of an active German battery*] with 2 rounds each time you hear crash in Courcelles area.' Such was the oddly unmilitary signal I sent Toc 2 at 6 PM, having no doubt been pressed by some aggrieved headquarter formation of New Zealand Division.

April 26   Two lighter events relieved a day of more serious shooting. At 3.25 PM Toc 5 fired 12 rounds at a camp beside Loupart Wood, Grévillers, and reported, 'Two tents obliterated and transport scattered.'[1] More credibly, between 6.45 PM and 6.55 PM Toc 3 fired 16 rounds at Germans repairing a road near Serre and reported, 'Party dispersed.'

May 5   LY 12, an unpleasantly resilient enemy battery, must have received a nasty surprise when all five batteries of the brigade were ordered to give it 2 salvoes per gun at 6.15 PM, and 1 further salvo at 6.30 PM. The number of rounds thus fired was 9, 12, 8, 12, and 12. Toc 3 were taken off this task before the final salvo and told to engage a battery which the F.O.O. at Tusculum saw firing from the north-west corner of Pendant Copse. 8 rounds were fired by Toc 3 on this new task.

[1] This story reached Corps Heavies, thence Corps Headquarters where a war correspondent swallowed it and telegraphed it home. It appeared in many papers. The range of the tents was about nine miles.

May 6   At 1.50 PM Toc 3 fired 15 rounds at German
            infantry which a New Zealand Company in the
front line said could be seen on a road beside the Ancre. The
result, reported by the New Zealanders and entered in the log
in the Colonel's writing, '5 O.K.s on road; enemy ran away
hard.'

May 7   In Benwell's writing: 'Programme GOLDFISH.
            Toc 1 may be called up by plane to fire on tanks
reputed to be on roads in L 26 b and L 27 a [*near Beauregard
Dovecote*]. Plane will send co-ordinates to battery. Battery to
report to us and continue, but we to tell them how much
ammunition to use. If line to battery goes dis [*disconnected,
i.e. fails*], they to carry on using discretion.'

GOLDFISH did not take place, no doubt because the tanks
had moved on.

May 8   In the Colonel's writing: 'PLUM. Battalion head-
            quarters at K 29 c 3.5 [*near Matthew Copse, Serre*].
Toc 4 can do this. 50 rounds and report if they want more.'

May 9   Also in the Colonel's writing: 'PLUM 5.30 PM.
            Ends 7.0 PM. 100 rounds. Very good results, many
O.K.s.'

May 11   In the Colonel's writing: 'EDITH. Toc 4 now
            firing at a machine-gun emplacement. 25 rounds
allowed and then to report.' And immediately below this
entry in Benwell's writing: 'EDITH ends 5.15 PM. 40 rounds.
4 O.K.s, many men scattered.'

May 14   Major Clark, the battery commander of Toc 4,
            was ebullient by nature, and the report in the
following entry, which is in Benwell's writing, sounds very like
his own words: '4.30 PM – 6.0 PM. Toc 4. Puisieux Church 40.
A large fire caused which lasted five minutes. Saw lots of Boche
who tried to put fire out. Toc 4 put over gas shell and Boches
ran hard as poss.'

May 16   In Benwell's writing: '6.45 PM. LY 16 Now Firing.
            12 Toc 4.' Below this the Colonel wrote: 'Not in
our area, should not have fired. Tell battery.'

[123]

May 17   Toc 5's roseate telescope was again in use at 3.48 PM
when, with observation from Tusculum, they fired
5 rounds at a camp 15,000 yards away – 12,000 yards or seven
miles from the observer – and reported, 'Men seen running
from tents.'

On the same day in the Colonel's writing: '6.15 PM. Toc 3.
LY 15. With balloon. 20 rounds. Balloon says All O.K.!!!!!!!'
No wonder the Colonel pencilled-in seven exclamation marks.

May 18   Two routine messages from Toc 1: '1.48 PM. How.
No. 467 KITCHENER 5 hours, buffer leaking.' and
'6.55 PM. How. No. 467 DERBY.'

Lloyd George features once in the log's pages too, but as a
code name for a shoot and not as a prime minister, vide a
message to Toc 1 in my writing: 'Do not use more than 25 on
LLOYD GEORGE.'

May 18/19 An unpleasant night which the Germans gave us
on our side of the line. In Benwell's writing:
'12.50 PM – 1.50 AM. 300 rounds mustard gas on Beaussart
from 4·2 guns.'

May 20   There is more probability than usual in Toc 5's
claim after firing 6 comparatively short-range
shots at 8.32 AM at movement observed near Miraumont:
'2 parties scattered, 2 men carried away.'

May 23   On this day Toc 5 reached the peak of their gun-
manship. At 6.45 PM they engaged a wireless station
at Serre, and after firing 5 rounds reported, 'Mast knocked
down.' And at 7.40 PM they fired 4 rounds at a train on the
light railway near Miraumont and reported, 'Smoke of train
and shell coincided.'

I should make it clear that many of the shoots detailed
above were mere frills, and as a typical example of the heavy
tasks which our batteries were carrying out day after
day I quote the following AERO (*observation by aeroplane*)

programme for May 26, received by us from Corps Heavies on the evening of May 25:

	Code call	Target	No. of rounds
Toc 1	BOX	LY 22 & LY 23	150 & 150
Toc 2	BUZ	LY 25	300
Toc 3	CAT	LY 15	300
Toc 4	FAN	Battery at L 26 a 8.3	300

It must not be thought that the batteries always got things their own way. They sustained steady casualties from enemy shelling, and at 2 AM on May 27 I notice an entry by Gardiner, in bed and half asleep to judge by his writing, 'Toc 3 and Toc 4 heavily gassed by batteries which Tusculum say firing from Grid 60° and Grid 120°. Ceased 3 AM on Toc 4, continued on Toc 3 from Grid 120° till 4 AM.'

In addition to Tusculum, which ranked as the brigade O.P. there were others made and manned by the different batteries, and on May 25 I see an entry in my writing: '10 PM. MARK O.P. pushed in. No one hurt.'

Throughout the later pages of the log counter-battery tasks predominate, and entries become correspondingly terser and less informative. More and more shoots were now being observed and corrected by plane, and from the number of guns being reported KITCHENER and from the reasons given, it is apparent that the gunners were not alone in suffering from the effects of overwork.

The final entry of human interest occurs on June 8, when at 7.5 PM Toc 2 fired 42 rounds at a ration party entering Serre and reported, 'Casualties, results excellent!' and I must not forget to mention the log's pages disclose that with a pencil in his hand the Colonel was sometimes a doodler.

CHAPTER XV

Storm in a Tin Mug

I have said before that the Colonel, a stickler about things that mattered – and about some that did not – wrote every order of importance in his own handwriting, and in words so precise, concise too, that no battery commander was likely to be in doubt as to what was required of him. There was one regrettable exception, and I shall tell of it now and of how it landed me in the only serious row I had with him.

Orders regarding battery moves, coming into the Secret category, were written in the book he kept solely for secret or confidential letters; this otherwise ordinary book had duplicate pages so that carbon copies could be made and preserved. Whenever I saw the book come out and the Colonel start writing in it, I prepared for the special ritual which I knew would surely follow. As soon as the actual writing had been completed the Colonel moistened his finger and tore out the top sheet or sheets; then, having moved on the carbon to lie sandwiched in readiness between the next two blank pages, he closed the book and put it away. Last he passed the order to me at the adjoining table to read and remember, and the matter had ended so far as he was concerned, for it was my responsibility to arrange early or immediate dispatch, and to see that the battery acknowledged promptly.

The order which caused the trouble was about a night move by Toc 1 to a new position – for a 9·2 battery a major affair with caterpillar tractors standing by to do the pulling, large earth boxes[1] to be emptied and refilled, and a score of lorries to shift the stores and ammunition – and the order was so framed that only one of the battery's several sections

[1] Each held two tons of earth.

would be out of action at the same time. The instruction which initiated this move had reached us from Corps Heavies an hour earlier, and I knew all about its complications because the Colonel had discussed them with me at some length.

No sooner had I read what the Colonel had written than it struck me that one small but vital paragraph referring to the location of the battery's new command post was ambiguous. As a lesser matter it passed through my mind that the activities of Gardiner's linesmen, who were responsible for the communications, were affected too.

The mistake I made was in telling the Colonel both these things; knowing exactly what he meant and wanted, it would have been better if I had said nothing and dealt with the situation behind the scenes.

It may be that the Colonel was more tired than usual, for we had been having a strenuous fortnight of S.O.S. shoots and moves and counter-moves because the front of the New Zealand Division – to whom we were now attached – was still fluid. He was undoubtedly more irritable, but I was not anticipating trouble since it was my responsibility to make sure the Colonel's orders were understood and acted upon, and it came as a shock when he said gruffy, "Those are my orders and don't quack. Get them off to Toc 1."

Knowing him as well as I did, I was aware that further argument was useless. "Yes, sir," I said, and handed the sheets to Fulton to register and seal.

I knew Toc 1's dispatch-rider was waiting outside for them. It will take him ten minutes to get back to his battery, I calculated; therefore within fifteen O.C. Toc 1 – Major Pargiter – will be telephoning for elucidation.

I made no mistake there. Sure enough my telephone buzzed.

"Adjutant here," I said as I picked up the receiver.

"O.C. Toc 1 here. About para. 6, little a, in your order. Is my command post to be located at – "

The Colonel's voice from his table broke in – the office in which we worked was half a Nissen hut, the other half being the mess. "Who are you speaking to?" he growled.

"O.C. Toc 1, sir."

"Is he asking about my order?"

"Yes, sir."

"Tell him to carry it out. And put the receiver down."

"Very good, sir," I replied, and to Pargiter I said, "The Colonel wishes his orders carried out. Unless you care to speak to him yourself, sir?"

"No, thank you." Pargiter's voice had stiffened.

I put the receiver back on the telephone and momentarily felt sorry that Toc 1 was involved instead of one of our other batteries. Not that, being in the Colonel's eyes a matter of principle, it was likely to have made the slightest difference, I told myself. Unhappily there was no love lost between the Colonel and O.C. Toc 1, a state of affairs which puzzled me since Pargiter was quite the best battery commander in the brigade, and that is saying a lot. He was a regular, he had come to us with both a wound and a mention in dispatches from an Indian mountain battery – a cachet similar to that of the Royal Horse Artillery – and to my certain knowledge he had all the qualities which Colonel Thorp expected to find, but rarely did find, in an officer. In addition he looked a soldier, and he was loved and respected by his battery. Yet Thorp did not like him, and I can only think his dislike was due to unconscious jealousy. On the reverse side it was as unhappily noticeable that Pargiter, a reserved and almost shy man, was rarely at his best either in the Colonel's presence or in speaking to him on the telephone.

So far as this incident had now gone, I felt uneasy and dissatisfied. From any angle I thought Pargiter justified, and the Colonel wrong. Yet what more could I do? The Colonel had nothing further to say on the subject, and I knew that with him the matter was closed. And after what had already happened it was improbable that Pargiter would get on a motor-cycle and come to headquarters in the hope of speaking to him. The minutes passed, and all of a sudden I made up my mind to do something. My day's work was over – it was long past supper-time – and I got up from my chair and said good night to the Colonel and went to my dug-out fifty yards away across the orchard.

There I lit my candle, buzzed on my dug-out telephone, and asked the switchboard operator for Toc 1.

A signaller of Toc 1 answered me, and I told him to tell Major Pargiter that the Adjutant wanted to speak to him.

Pargiter soon came on. "I'm so sorry about what happened ten minutes ago," I said. "I'm in my dug-out now and can tell you what that para. means. Your command post's to be at the first lot of co-ordinates, not the second. I know that because I was with the Colonel and he talked about it before he wrote—"

The candle guttered in a draught. My dug-out door had opened, and the Colonel, standing in the doorway, asked, "Who's that you're speaking to?"

"Major Pargiter, sir,"

"Did he telephone to you, or you to him?"

"I to him, sir,"

"What about?"

"To explain para. 6(a) of your order, sir."

"Did I not tell you not to speak to him?"

"You did, sir."

"They why have you disobeyed me?"

"Because Major Pargiter did not know what he was expected to do."

Grim-faced and shaking with anger, the Colonel said, "I will not have a disobedient Adjutant. You will pack your valise and leave me tomorrow morning."

My temper went to the skies too. "I don't mind telling you I'd disobey you again if the circumstances were the same. I tried to tell you about your order, but you wouldn't let me. I think you're an unreasonable and obstinate man, and I think you're being unfair to Major Pargiter. To his battery too. That's all I've got to say, sir – except that I'll be glad to leave you."

Surprisingly the Colonel took my salvoes in silence and departed without another word.

I lit a cigarette and sat down on my bed. I too was very angry and not in the least sorry for what I had said. In the candlelight I stared at my accumulated possessions – the

I   [129]

chair made by the late Gunner Freshwater, the new book-case I had just knocked up from the timbers of Mailly-Maillet church – and decided some must be left behind. Stumping out my cigarette and throwing the end into my 5·9 cartridge case of nicely polished brass, I next decided I would ask the Colonel to post me to Toc 1 because I liked them all and so admired Pargiter. . . . My successor here would probably be Benwell. . . . Well, he was welcome to the job. And perhaps his temperament was better suited to it than mine. . . .

My dug-out door again burst open, and this time my visitor was Gardiner. He arrived in a hurry – he lived in a state of hurry except when in bed – to say how sorry he was to hear I was going and how much he'd miss me. It was unnecessary to ask him how he knew; his switchboard operators had trained ears and throughout my conversation with the Colonel I must have kept the telephone receiver in my hand.

Immediately after his departure I undressed and went to bed. Let tomorrow take care of itself, all other tomorrows too, I was thinking, and to my annoyance just before I fell asleep the telephone buzzed. It was Major Pargiter. Sparing of words as ever, he said, "The move's under way and I want to thank you for your help. I hope I haven't caused trouble at your end."

"Nothing to speak of, sir," I replied.

The following morning I got up early, and when Donaldson came with my shaving water I told him to dismantle my bed and pack my valise as soon as he had breakfasted. He was a kindly Lowland Scot and an excellent batman; he said nothing nor did his face register any emotion. Then I followed the path round the edge of the orchard to the men's dug-outs to ask Fulton to do his best for my successor and not to cut off his nose to spite his face by asking for a posting himself. He said all at headquarters would be sorry to see me go – even, he thought, Captain Vincent.

It was still twenty minutes short of breakfast time, and I returned to my dug-out and started to collect my things for packing. My door opened yet again, and in came the Colonel's head and half his body. Under his greatcoat he was still in pyjamas; there were gumboots on his feet, and behind his spectacles his unshaven face looked so old and worn that I almost felt sorry for him. "Unpack your valise," he told me gruffly. "I'm not changing Adjutants."

It was the nearest approach to an apology of which he was capable, and I accepted it as such. "Right, sir," I said, and added to his departing back, "I'm glad to stay, sir."

Ten minutes later I went in to breakfast. He was alone in the mess, drinking his tin mug of tea – he rarely ate anything for breakfast. He finished in silence and went through to his table and began looking through the file of signals and messages sent in by the night duty officer from his dug-out.

"Have you finished your breakfast?" he called impatiently. "There are several messages here to be attended to."

I got up from the breakfast table – it had a covering of once-white American cloth, I remember – and took the file from him. There were all the usual things including the night's list of casualties and about urgently-needed fuses and ammunition and missing lorries and faulty recuperators, and there was even one from Toc 1 reporting 4 guns DERBY (*in action*). As I picked up my telephone it struck me that the switchboard operator who answered as I asked to be put through to Siege Park would be justified in feeling considerable surprise.

So, like the couple in the fairy tale, the Colonel and I lived happily ever after – or fairly happily, because he could still be difficult at times. He bore me no ill will, nor I him, and, outwardly at any rate, the relationship between us remained unchanged. But on my side I was conscious of a slight, very slight, feeling of moral superiority. It was almost as though I had graduated. And as for the Colonel, I could not help noticing that henceforward, before passing it over to me, he scrutinized any written order even more meticulously than had been his custom in the past.

As a tail-piece to this story I should mention that as a result of his only fault – his sleeping-in habits – Gardiner got into trouble too. Admittedly there were times when he had to do a fair amount of out-of-door night-work, but, as I told him more than once, he was only annoying the Colonel by trying to take advantage of it. I also pointed out that the Colonel, though a bachelor, was well aware no doctor gets called to a confinement every night.

In the end the Colonel got more than annoyed. One morning a quarter of an hour after the breakfast table should have been cleared and Gardiner had not appeared, I saw him writing away in that special book, and when he had finished he tore off the top sheet and handed it to me. "Get this delivered at once," he ordered.

This is what he had written, and I am not relying on memory because I liked his letter so much that I made, kept, and still have, a copy of it:

CONFIDENTIAL   90 BRIGADE
                                      R.G.A.

Lieut. A. N. Gardiner

                                      22/634

You are to get up at such an hour in the morning as to ensure finishing your breakfast not later than 8.50 AM. You are to start your day's work not later than 9.0 AM.

Should you at any time fail to obey this order you are to report in writing to the Adjutant 90 Brigade R.G.A. giving the reasons for doing so.

A. H. THORP Lt. Col. R.G.A.
30.5.18.   O.C. 90 Brigade R.G.A.

No report was received by the Adjutant because Gardiner did not fail again, and it could well be that the Colonel was a better psychologist than any of us knew.

CHAPTER XVI

Doing Their Best

One bizarre incident of that summer still at times disturbs my dreams, and it came about because the service we had been getting from the local kite-balloon section was poorer than we felt it should be. Here let me explain that kite-balloons was a branch, albeit a lowly one, of the Royal Flying Corps, and it was their job, wind and clouds permitting and whenever no co-operation plane was available for us, to observe our shoots and correct them by means of telephone messages relayed from the sky to our battery command posts. The local section was commanded by a stout-hearted ex-R.F.C. pilot named Hoppy Cleaver, so called because he had only one leg. Everyone liked him, but no one thought much of his balloons – or of balloonatics generally, as observers were known behind their backs.

One morning the Colonel summoned him to brigade headquarters to hear our complaints. Business at our brigade was invariably conducted in the office, not over a beer or whisky in the mess, and Hoppy Cleaver, having listened politely to the Colonel's string of grumbles, said, "I accept some of what you say, sir. But your shoots are mostly counter-battery shoots, which mean your targets are usually a map reference anything up to four or five miles from the chap in the balloon. I wonder if one of your officers could come up with us, and I think he'll soon see it's not quite as easy as many people on the ground seem to think."

The Colonel thought that a good idea. "Order a battery to detail an officer to go up," he said to me.

"May I go myself, sir?" I asked – not through desire but because I had so often been the unwilling post office for the batteries' complaints.

The Colonel nodded agreement, and after thanking Cleaver for his visit in a minimum number of words – four, I seem to remember – turned to other things.

"Good man," said Cleaver as I went to see him off in his car. "Come tomorrow at two o'clock and I'll take you up myself."

When I arrived the following afternoon the balloon was close-hauled and swaying uneasily in the breeze. Its basket, a few feet above my head, was swaying too. The balloon was attached to its winch by a slender cable of steel wire, and the winch was bolted to the floor of a lorry which, though mobile, looked substantial enough to allay my passing fears that it might rise from the earth and follow the balloon into the air. Two men in R.F.C. uniform were standing by at the winch, and one of them showed me how to fit the harness of a folded parachute to my back.

It was a sunny afternoon, a particularly beautiful one on account of the number of small fleecy white clouds between us and the clear blue sky, and Cleaver glanced at them as we were clambering into the basket. "One thousand feet," he ordered the winch corporal. "No smoking, mind," he said to me.

There were no further preliminaries. The winch began to hum, and up we went. Cleaver turned to me. "The visibility's perfect, I know," he said. "But all these low clouds are an invitation to any lurking Hun. Sorry about that because I wanted to take you up to fifteen hundred."

The basket was made of wicker and its sides breast high. Inside there was just room for the two of us to stand upright; the equipment consisted of a telephone, an aneroid barometer, and a compass.

Our rate of ascent if slow seemed steady, and we were soon out of earshot of the winch gear. An upward glance reassured me that the balloon looked more than large enough to take good care of me, and I gazed downward. The cable appeared woefully thin, and it needed a real effort to take my eyes from it. By now the winch was a couple of hundred feet below, and I could see the white blobs of the winchmen's faces each time they looked up to watch our progress. Having reached the conclusion that if the cable parted there was nothing anyone could do about it, I took my Zeiss glasses from their case and slung them round my neck. Here, compared with my only previous experience of the air – in a Nieuport monoplane – there was an unpleasant sense of insecurity. When sitting in an aeroplane the sense of detachment is complete, but standing in an airborne basket seemed neither one thing nor the other. The wretched cable still made us part of the ground, and that was the first of several times that afternoon I felt sorry for balloonatics.

At six hundred feet we were free of most earthly noises, and again I looked down. For the first time I saw the front line as it really was, mile upon mile of it. Now running straight, now turning this way or that in an apparently haphazard and unnecessary curve, now straight again, it stretched roughly north and south till it vanished in both directions in sheer distance. The depth and complexity of the German trench system surprised me, and of the opposing belts of wire, dull brown and rusting, there was considerably more on the German side than on ours. No Man's Land, much wider in places than I had realized from any map, looked like a long-neglected race-course by reason of the distinctive greenness of its bare but relatively undisturbed turf. To me it was like one of those bird's-eye drawings so popular in the illustrated weeklies of that time, except that no artist had conveniently inserted place-names alongside the more famous strong points and ruined townships of the Somme.

Far behind in enemy territory I saw factories with smoking chimneys and pleasantly normal villages, and the view was so extensive that I counted six streaks or plumes of steam from the engines of equally normal trains. The winch was now so tiny that it was hardly visible, and only the glint of the nearest couple of hundred feet of cable reminded me that we were still connected to the ground. It was such a good day for visibility that every balloonatic, British and German alike, seemed to be taking the air; north and south I counted twenty-three balloons, all lined up at regular intervals of say a mile and a half and all apparently suspended in nothing. There was comfort in numbers, I thought. And no wonder they were called sausage-balloons, I thought too.

Artillery was active on both sides of the line, on the whole a curiously silent activity, though by some acoustic freak occasional booms reached our ears. Yet the landscape was alive with the puffs of bursting shells and the gun flashes of batteries in action, and, like matches being struck in the opposite stand at a football match, the brief glow of some newly-created fire.

All of a sudden the motion, or more correctly the lack of it, changed. In sympathy with the balloon the basket began to tug and sway and swing in what must have been quite a wind. I looked at Hoppy Cleaver but he did not seem concerned; with his glasses to his eyes and his elbows on the edge of the basket to steady himself he was studying something behind the German lines. I understood what had happened.

We had reached our height, the winch was no longer letting out cable, and the balloon was so to speak anchored. This is devilish unpleasant, I thought, and wondered how soon it would be before I was sick. After looking down the cable and finding no palliative there I copied Cleaver by raising my glasses, but through the motion of the basket I found it hard to keep them fixed on any given spot.

Hoppy Cleaver laid the folded part of his parachute over the edge of the basket and indicated to me to do likewise; then, picking up the telephone, he said into it, "Tell the battery we're ready now."

The shoot of 300 rounds we were about to observe was being fired by Toc 1; I had chosen it in preference to the afternoon shoots of our 6-inch batteries because I imagined 9·2 bursts would be that much easier to see. Their target was a 5·9 battery engaged by us several times before and known for its viciousness no less than for its recuperative powers.

"See the target area all right?" Cleaver asked, and I admitted I didn't.

"You will if you look in the right direction. Try ten degrees left of where you're looking now."

I did. "Afraid I still can't get it," I said at last.

"I'll show you on the map first," said Cleaver kindly, one hand holding the receiver to his ear. "Here. Agreed? . . . Now look where I'm pointing – never mind the basket turning, you'll soon get used to that – and you'll see the grey smoke of a train, it's probably burning wood. Got it? . . . Two fingers left there's a house with its windows catching the sun. . . . Good. And half a mile in front of that there's a small roundish wood quite by itself. Got that too? . . . Running across the front edge of the wood there's a sunken road – you can't see it but it's there all right – and the hostile battery's just beside it. It's in it, in fact – 'No. 1 fired!' "

By using the edge of the basket I managed to steady my glasses on the front of the wood, and twenty seconds later Cleaver said, "Did you get it?"

"No."

"Outside the field of your glasses, I expect. It was short." He telephoned a correction. . . . 'No. 2 fired!' "

I saw that one. From the faint blur of smoke it had landed plumb in the wood, but owing to the distance and the jerking basket I could not for the life of me judge whether it was over, right, or both. Hoppy Cleaver knew, and another crisp correction was telephoned down.

Half a dozen more rounds fell one after another, all more or less visible.

"I'm no damned good at this," I said. "I see them all right, but from this low angle of sight I can't say if they're out for line or for elevation."

"They're all O.K. for line. 1 and 3 are still shooting short, all the others are a bit over."

More corrections, and rounds began to fall in and around the target area.

"They've hit something," from me. "That's some of their ammunition going up."

Ranging ended, and Toc 1 proceeded to gunfire of 50

[137]

rounds per gun. As a result the target area, half the wood too, became obscured by smoke. There were three more fires, and it seemed clear that Toc I was giving that German battery hell.

By now I felt quite at home in the basket, and there was so much of interest in the world above and below that all fears of sickness were forgotten. Through my glasses the fleecy clouds were lovely, and from them I looked north, then south – "My God, what's that?" I asked.

A balloon – the fourth from us – was emitting oily black smoke. Then it sagged, and the whole of it burst into bright red flame. The volume of black smoke soared and became tremendous.

The swaying of our basket ceased because the winchmen had seen it too – we were being hauled down.

"There's the Hun that did it!" I said, still watching through my glasses. "He's tackling the next one now."

Its occupants had not waited. Two tumbling bodies. Then two parachutes opened and floated gently earthwards. An anti-aircraft battery opened up, its white burst dotting the sky at the right height. Otherwise its shells were absurdly wide of the mark. The Taube, unworried by them, came on in a leisurely if determined way and set the next balloon alight in exactly the same way as the first. I was relieved to see he did not dive to shoot up the parachutists. By this time the first balloon, or what was left of it, was dropping like a blazing paper bag.

Still unperturbed, the Hun came on to the second from us. I could see his swift tracer bullets going into it, and then I heard the sharp rat-tat-tat of his machine-gun. It too went up in smoke and flame, and down it came more quickly than the others. The Taube was skilful in avoiding it, but it was touch and go if it would catch up the two parachutists.

The next balloon to us was, like ourselves, perceptibly lower. But nothing like low enough, and as the Hun came on towards it I saw its two balloonatics scramble over the edge of the basket and drop. Both parachutes opened, but one seemed to take a long time about it.

Hoppy Cleaver was now standing on the edge of our own basket, and I saw him tighten his harness and finger the release-box. "Mind the cable when you jump," he said to me.

Finding it hard to choose between watching him and the Hun plane, I settled for the latter and saw it set alight our nearest neighbour as easily and quickly as the previous three. Then, skirting the smoke and flame, it flew on in our direction. I felt a totally different kind of detachment. This can't mean me, I thought. I looked to see if Cleaver was still there; to my surprise he was getting back into the basket and I remember thinking for a one-legged man he was remarkably nimble. He was looking at me, I remember too. I glanced again at the Hun. Still tailed by the hot but inaccurate fire of two if not three anti-aircraft batteries, he had turned away and was streaking for home.

Cleaver said, "He must have run out of incendiary. All the same four balloons in one sortie isn't bad going."

During the rest of the haul-down we did not speak, and when we reached the ground neither of the winchmen who helped us out so much as grinned.

"Come into the mess and have a drink," Cleaver said. "I don't know about you but I could do with one myself."

"Tell me, why did you get back into the basket?" I asked. "Before the Hun turned off, I mean."

"To throw you out, of course. You were my guest, and I knew you hadn't the sense or guts to get out yourself."

What he said was true.

"But don't you worry about it," he was saying. "And anyway you'll be able to tell your Colonel we balloonatics always do our best."

CHAPTER XVII

The War is Ending

The war, now in its fifth summer, was ending, but we were not yet conscious of it. We and the French and the Germans were equally war-weary, and each of us knew only too well the meaning of the words 'scraping the bottom of the barrel.' Thus, however vehemently I might have denied it forty years ago, it was the Americans we had to thank for victory in 1918, for without them the war might have continued for several more years and ended inconclusively. Apart from their capacity to give as well as take severe casualties, their very presence – and in such numbers – knocked what stuffing was left out of the Germans and put fresh heart into the French and ourselves. No one in the line could fail to observe that from August onwards the Germans, though still tough and brave, were no longer the fighters they had been.

At brigade headquarters we met our first Americans during the early part of the summer, two or three quiet and earnest men quite unlike the boastful types Americans were generally believed to be. They were gunner officers, sent to learn how we did things and to profit from our experience, and if at the beginning of their visit they may have thought there was little we could teach them they quickly saw their mistake.

On our own front – the Ancre – the final offensive opened on August 21. We were still with IV Corps; its Divisions consisted of the 5th (recently returned from Italy), the 37th, 42nd, and New Zealand, and on the first day the Germans were attacked along the whole Corps front from Bucquoy to Beaumont Hamel. Two of Toc 4's hows. went forward on tanks, an exciting innovation which must have startled one or two German artillery regiments by the valuable counter-battery work which was thus performed. We were with the New Zealanders on August 29 when they recaptured Bapaume. The brigade's line of advance was some miles south of the line along which we had retreated, and on September 8 – a date I remember because it was my twenty-third birthday – I borrowed a dispatch-rider's motor-cycle and went to see our old headquarters at Beugny. I did not linger there long; when I opened the door – the same old door – of my dug-out I found it filled with a blackening heap of German dead.

Walker, a young subaltern who had come to the brigade from England six weeks before the retreat and whom Pargiter – among his other qualities a good judge of men – had picked for Toc 1, has surely hit the nail on the head. We have become lifelong friends, and recently while talking about those days he said, "Advancing is never so pleasant as retreating. There were all the smells and all the unburied corpses, and one tended to outrun supplies – no salt, no whisky, and sometimes only biscuit with the bully because there was no bread."

But to return to my dug-out for a moment or two. It had been a particularly good one, constructed of several sets of steel elephants lowered into a hole dug from the high roadbank. It was floored with sleepers stolen from the near-by Bapaume-Cambrai railway line, and the signals corporal – a one-time ship's painter – had painted the interior with two coats of white paint given to me by the Corps camouflage officer for other purposes. On the back wall one of our dispatch-riders had built a splendid fireplace with bricks from Beugny village, and he had added a hearth made of tiles from Beugny church. Front and back the inside was lined with wood which one of the telephonists, a peacetime decorator, had covered with green canvas. The door came from Beugny too. The window had a wide sill of old oak; the dug-out's finishing touch was a beautifully carved over-mantel, also from the ruins of Beugny. I had furnished it with a table and a rug bought in Amiens and a lamp from Albert, and thanks to Gardiner it was on the telephone.

An R.E. construction officer who saw it was so impressed that on his following visit he brought a pane of glass for the window. On its outside the rounded tops of the steel elephants, which just protruded over the roadbank, had been covered with growing turf. The window frame was lined in green and black. The bank on either side of the door was neatly revetted with corrugated iron, and a sunken duckboard led from the doorstep to the road. I occupied it for three months, and until March 21 no shell fell nearer than five hundred yards away. I make no excuse for living in such luxury or for attempting to make the impermanent permanent; I had merely remembered and acted upon the advice given to us by our brigadier before Gallipoli, "Be as comfortable as you can for as long as you can."

In the next two months we advanced thirty or forty miles. We kept just south of Cambrai, and our route was by Ruyaulcourt, Briastre, and Solesmes to Salesches, a wretched village four miles south-west of the walled and moated town of Le Quesnoy, which the New Zealanders stormed on November 4. Hatch, the signal officer of Toc 1, was killed at Briastre by a chance shell which hit him in the back. He was the youthful and charming regular ex-ranker who had won the M.M., D.C.M., and M.C., and only the other day I learned – from his signals corporal, a Liverpool friend of mine – that when he was posted to the battery in its early days the men sensed that the officers of that time did not welcome the arrival of an ex-ranker in their mess.

More happily, I am reminded by Walker of an incident which occurred at Solesmes; it is worth telling on account of the light it throws on the character of two of our battery commanders. A IV Corps Order issued on October 20 stressed that no village was to be bombarded with heavy artillery unless it had been previously determined that all its civilian inhabitants had been evacuated, and at lunchtime the following day Major Clark, battery commander of Toc, 4 bounced into Toc 1's mess and smilingly announced in tones of simulated fear, "I say, Pargiter, I've just done a most frightful thing! You know that big factory in E 19 ack? Well, I was registering my guns on it an hour ago when it suddenly burst into flames and simply disappeared. I do hope they won't make me pay for it. . . . Still, not bad shooting, don't you think?"

Shortly afterwards Major Strover, the new battery commander of Toc 2, strode into the mess too. He was a regular, a disciplinarian and a pessimist but a good man. "Afternoon, Pargiter," he said, more gloomy than usual. "My battery did a very unlucky registration this morning. We were shooting at the factory in E 19 ack, and we set it on fire. Rather unfortunate, I'm afraid."

That same evening the intelligence supplement of the New Zealand Division's Daily Summary stated: 'At 10.45 this morning the factory in E 19 a was seen to be on fire and is still burning. It was probably destroyed by the enemy as there was no shelling in the vicinity at the time.'

I have already spoken of the Colonel's passion for Salvage, and the depth of his feelings on the subject sometimes came as a shock to those who did not know him very well. The last occasion when Toc 1 went into action as a complete battery was on the near or west bank of the River Selle – there had just been quite a fierce battle for its crossings – and the Colonel on his morning rounds arrived to see that one of their guns had been erected on top of a length of telephone wire. He promptly summoned the duty officer – Walker, as it happened – pointed to the wire which had all but disappeared in the mud, and asked what it was doing there. "Oh, it's only an old bit and it's not in use, sir," Walker began cheerfully, and it is true that a party of New Zealanders repairing the road fifty yards away downed tools and stood listening to what the Colonel said to him.

A few days before the Armistice the infantry of IV Corps drove the Germans from the great Mormal Forest; the roads which passed through it were so few and so poor that for the first time in our existence the guns of the brigade were unable to follow up. Toc 2 contrived to send forward two hows. which were in action in the middle of the Forest on November 6 and 7, and the Colonel himself helped to haul No. 2 into position, the last of the brigade's guns to fire a round in the war. The bridges over the Sambre had been destroyed, and no further advance proved possible.

Thus November 11 found the majority of us still at Salesches – ten or more miles behind our infantry and at least twenty from the nearest Germans – and a small group of officers assembled outside the Adjutant's office and greeted eleven o'clock with a half-hearted cheer. We had no beer, no gin, no cigarettes.

A day or two later General Russell sent the Colonel a farewell letter of which we were so proud that I print it in full:

> All good things come to an end, and amongst others the association of the New Zealand Division with IV Corps and consequently with 90th Brigade.
>
> It has been, as times go, a long partnership and a successful one. We shall carry away with us none but pleasant memories and sincere admiration for the work done by you and your Brigade. I do not know how it came about, but we have had closer personal touch and more confidence in you and your guns than at any time since the Division has been in France.
>
> I hope you will let your men know this, and that this expression on my part is not merely a courtesy between one unit and another but the feeling of every man in the ranks.

I went to say goodbye to General Russell myself, and he asked me why I didn't come out to New Zealand to settle and told me to let him know if I did. I have often thought how different my life would have been if I had followed his suggestion; in the early nineteen-twenties there were occasions when I felt sorry I had not.

The weeks which followed the Armistice were slow and stagnant, and to make them worse we remained at Salesches till we knew every smell by heart. As an escape I went one day to Mons, rapidly becoming a favourite sightseeing centre for the British Army by virtue of being the nearest town of any size left by the Germans as a going concern. Up to now my mental picture of a sugar factory was that of most other soldiers – a large ruin sprawling dangerously close to cross-roads, its heaps of rubble as often as not used as an observation post by us, by the Germans as an artillery ranging point. But in Mons I saw one with workers hurrying in and out, cart-loads of sugar beet being tossed into little pens in the yard, and clouds of steam escaping from the boiler house. The windows of the toy shops were interesting too. They were filled with German toys, specially clockwork U-boats and Zeppelins and Gothas. There were toy soldiers as well, British, French, and German, all obviously made in Germany, and needless to say the German soldiers were all lying on their little grey backs with the notice KAPUT displayed beside them. German postage stamps overprinted BELGIEN were for sale as souvenirs, and many shopkeepers seemed unable to remember that the currency of Mons was no longer to be reckoned in marks. For our part it was hard to grasp that two weeks previously Germans had been eating in the same restaurants, using the same spoons and forks, being served by the same waiters, sending home hand-made lace bought in the same shops – though probably not at the same high prices.

Throughout my day in Mons the big square, packed as it was with countless returning evacuees, each family surrounded by bundles of bedding and patiently awaiting any lorry which would help them on their way, resembled an open railway station. I spoke to an elderly refugee about things in general, and he told me that the quantity of our artillery and the quality of our *car-autos* (lorries) amazed him and his family most. In the later afternoon I made a pilgrimage to Nimy Bridge, two miles north, where the 4th Battalion of The Royal Fusiliers had taken the first shock of the Battle of Mons. I must say I found it disappointing in some ways; there were no trenches to be seen or inspected, and the small houses which lined both banks of the Canal looked undamaged. Night had come when I returned to

K

Mons; its gay and brilliantly-lighted streets made the greatest impression of all.

As for us in Salesches, the sudden transition from war to peace proved more irksome than anyone had imagined, and even the Colonel, faced with nothing left to salve, found little that mattered to do. He was still out on his rounds one morning when the rest of us sat down to lunch, and Gardiner started filling the tin mugs with gin – a mistake which was easy enough to make since we often used empty gin and whisky bottles as water bottles. The gin was poured back once the mistake was discovered, but we resolved to leave the Colonel's mug as it was and say nothing. He came in and sat down, and soon he raised it and began to drink. The faint look of puzzled surprise which first crossed his face changed quickly into a brief beatific smile which as quickly passed away, and his expression became as impassive as ever as he continued drinking till the mug was empty. He did not say a word, either then or later. Was his silence due to reluctance to lose face by conceding that for once we had pulled his leg? Or could it be that he liked a quarter of a pint of neat gin for lunch but felt unable to admit it?

He surprised us in a different way by displaying unexpected talents not previously mentioned because so few had known of their existence. He was a first-class mimic, and to witness him performing his song and dance act to a spellbound battery audience and listen to him singing in an authentic Cockney accent – with all the appropriate capers too – *My Old Dutch* or *We Knocked 'em in the Old Kent Road* and other coster songs of Albert Chevalier was an experience which no one fortunate enough to be a member of his audience could ever forget. With his stunted body and his bow legs he looked the part too, and on those rare occasions when he could be persuaded to take off his tunic and remove his spectacles, don an old French cap borrowed from heaven knows whom, and mount the improvised platform and begin to sing, it was no wonder that he soon brought down the house in delighted cheers.

[146]

A week before Christmas we had to say goodbye to Toc 1, whom we were ordered to leave behind, and we trekked by road via Le Quesnoy, Bavai, Maubeuge, and Mons to Genappe, a friendly and hospitable town half-way between Charleroi and Brussels. Here demobilization set in, and as a railwayman I was among the first to go. Graham had succeeded Benwell as Orderly Officer, and I handed over to him and returned to England and the London & North Western Railway. They sent me to help in running the railway side of the demobilization centre at Prees Heath in Shropshire, and there was I in civilian life and earning £120 a year.

I am not ashamed to confess that I look back upon my time with the 90th Brigade in Flanders and France as by far the most fulfilling eighteen months of my life. My home ties were slight, and I was neither married nor engaged. I had an absorbing job, responsibility well beyond my years, the companionship and friendship of men better and older than myself, and days if not weeks of excitement which often, yet not too often, were spiced with danger.[1] No man in his early twenties can ask for more.

[1] I have no record of the total casualties suffered by the Brigade since its formation in December 1917, but Toc 3's figures will serve as a yardstick. 277 Siege Battery R.G.A. arrived in France early in 1917, and during twenty months of active service its losses amounted to 70 killed and 120 wounded. Of its original 7 officers only Mills and Worrall were still present on Armistice Day; officer turnover had been 30. The battery had incurred most of its casualties in the Third Battle of Ypres, and not while with us.

CHAPTER XVIII

Reprise

In the winter of 1921 I found myself in Bruges – I was travelling from Germany to Spain. I am fond of Bruges, which I like to fancy is not unlike the old Ypres, and there I saw an Australian soldier. Blouse tunic, slouch hat, polished brown boots, nails squeaking on the pavé, I can see and hear him yet. I suppose that he like myself was sightseeing; we passed several times. He was swaggering through the streets with a true Australian roll, and people were turning to stare. We did not speak, but he had fanned the flame which Bruges with its Flemish names and clattering clogs and old familiar smells had already kindled.

I returned to my hotel and packed my bag. By stealing an extra day I felt sure it could be done. The railway guide showed me how – I must spend that night in Lille.

I left Bruges in the late afternoon; it was soon too dark to see more of Flanders than the flatness and the poplars. There was an hour to wait at Roulers . . . Roulers, here was a name to conjure with. How often, aeroplane photograph in hand, had I steadied my magnifying glass over the station to see if the 9·2 gun on the railway spur by Poperinghe had done the damage its owner – a friend of the Colonel – claimed. . . . And here was I eating a pork chop in the station hotel.

At six next morning I was up. There was some difficulty in persuading the night porter that I had paid my bill overnight, I remember, but by seven I was sitting in the overheated Paris express. At Arras I changed into the *train omnibus* which served all stations to Amiens. My zero hour was approaching, and already I began to feel childishly excited. My destination was Beugny, a village of no importance to anyone but me. It lay some five miles from Bapaume along the Cambrai road, and to reach it I learned I must take the light railway from Achiet-le-Grand.

Achiet had not changed much in four years, I decided. The mud and the railway lines looked just the same, and I walked into the road half expecting to see Thompson waiting with the brigade car.

"I hope you had a good leaf, sir?" he would have said with his staid grin.

"Tophole, thanks," – we said 'tophole' in those days – I would have replied. "Anything new up the line?"

And he would have answered, "Jerry's been quiet these last few days though he was dropping a few into Morchies on Tuesday, you could hear them quite plain. And I did hear 95 Battery had two or three wounded."

And by now I would have been sitting in the Vauxhall, and Thompson would have let in the clutch with a jerk – he often did that when the Colonel wasn't present – and twenty minutes later we would have been in Beugny. The Colonel would have been seated in the office with the map board before him.

"Hullo. You back?" he would have growled. "Help me with these pin-points, there's a good fellow. . . ."

But, alas, the only car to be seen was an old Ford which muddily announced it was for hire at 40 francs an hour or 200 for the whole day, and I turned back into the station and bought a ticket.

My train was waiting. It consisted of three small and remarkably uncomfortable carriages, and it was nearly full. A number of parcels and packages and hens in crates and animals in sacks were thrown from the platform into the van, and off we went. I stood on the little platform at the tail end of the last carriage, but the tantalizing morning mists – the same old mists – were down, and I could hardly see a thing.

It was through my ears I first became aware how times had changed. We had pulled up in the mist. There were some dim buildings, and the guard ran up and down shouting, "BeeveeYAY! BeeveeYAY!" What was he saying? Trying to tell me that Biefvillers was no longer known as Beef

Villas? . . . It was hard to believe, perhaps because I did not wish to believe. . . . None the less it was true.

On again. The mists were lifting. This bit of country looked familiar, and we stopped a second time. "FRAY-meecour! FRAYmeecour!" the guard was shouting now – Frémicourt. . . . But, FRAYmeecour or Fremmycourt, it was the same little hamlet in which the headquarters of 51st and 56th Divisions had lived during our time. Here one fine morning I had gone in best bib and tucker to apologize to an angry Divisional Commander because one of our gunners, less soldierly than many, when ordered to fire a musketry course on the borrowed divisional range, had shot a Black Watch sergeant through the arm. . . . A peculiarly unsporting shot too, I had not dared to add to the Divisional Commander, since the sergeant had been sleeping in his tent.

And so we came to Beugny. I dismounted from the train and looked about me with doubting eyes. 'Beugny-le-Château,' the station board insisted. And now there was a Café de la Gare outside the station gates. I had not break-fasted, and I entered. I asked for an omelette, but there were no eggs. *San fairy ann,* coffee and bread and jam would do. While I was waiting for it I inspected the rack of postcards by the door. Yes, they confirmed it – 'Beugny-le-Château.'

"Why 'le-Château'?" I asked Madame.

"Why not? Before the war there was a château here."

"Never!"

"But yes, m'sieu. Only a small one, it is true."

"Where?" I asked, still incredulous.

"Beside the church."

I drank my coffee in silence. How could my halting French explain that the Beugny we knew was so flat that few of us discovered even the church?

I paid my bill and hurried through the village to brigade headquarters. The sunken lane began as muddily as ever, the torn tree-stumps at the corner greeted me as sadly. On the site of our stables a small house had been erected; its owner was working in his garden and I felt inclined to tell him that by digging down eigthteen inches below his front door he might find the mortal remains of Jenny the cable-cart horse, killed early in the morning of March 21.

Our garage had gone, but the heap of chalk beside it – spoil from the mined dug-out – remained. Our line of shacks in the roadbank had gone too. I remembered that they had been dismantled by the Germans during the summer of '18, but it was easy to identify the scars where once they had stood – the Colonel's, the Doc's, the Sergeant-major's, mine. Mine, as snug a home as I had had during the war, was filled with rubbish consisting of stones, a rusting tangle of barbed wire, shell cases, steel helmets of both sides, blown tins once containing bully beef.

I walked on, searching the roadbank for the mined dug-out. But both entrances had vanished without trace; no doubt with the removal of the supporting timber the shafts had collapsed during the winter rains. A haycock had been put beside the ruins of the office hut, and another was standing on the near crest beyond – in full view of the Hindenburg Line.

The roadway itself had been re-metalled, and I could find no evidence of the shell holes of March 21. There was nothing else to see, I felt, and I scrambled up the bank and struck across the open for Morchies, as I had done many times before. The grass seemed as tough and as rank; there was the same clean smell of damp winter earth. The contours of the ridges before me looked the same, and Beugny, a quarter of a mile away to my right, seemed its misty self.

The day was very quiet, but there had been many similar days during the winter months of 1917. A light breeze was blowing from the east, and instinctively I tuned my ears to catch the slow whistle and the distant echoing crash which announced the arrival of yet another 5·9 in Lagnicourt or Doignies or Beaumetz. . . . But all I heard was the crowing of a cock in Beugny, followed by the shrill laughter of a child.

I reached a patch of newly ploughed earth where the going was so heavy that I turned back towards Beugny. Soon I came upon the Lagnicourt road a couple of hundred yards above the position of our battery of 6-inch guns. The pits were still there; so, strangely enough, were dozens of empty cartridge tins. How furious the Colonel would have been.

"Fetch the officer on duty," he would have commanded the nearest gunner, and no doubt old Jobling would have come gently forward – 'old,' I see I have called a man of not quite forty.

"What the dickens are all these empties doing here, Mr Jobson?" the Colonel would have demanded in a voice shaking with indignation – he was bad at remembering names.

"They're w-waiting for the l-lorry to collect them, sir," Jobling would have stuttered without a turn of his thin red hair. "I l-left them l-like this to camouflage them in case a Boche p-plane came over."

A postman on a bicycle overtook me as I left the battery position for the village.

"*Bonjour, m'sieu!*" he called gaily; they were friendly in those parts that day.

"*Bonjour!*" I replied as gaily. "There is a post office in Beugny now?"

"No, the nearest is in Vaulx." He was pointing. "It is three kilometres over there."

"I know that all right."

"What did you say?" He had now dismounted from his bicycle.

"I was just saying that things have altered since I was last here."

From Beugny I walked along the Cambrai road towards the line. A lorry laden with bricks and tiles overtook me and splashed me with mud. There was nothing very new about that, I reflected, watching it bump past the spot where the board saying:

NO VEHICULAR TRAFFIC
BEYOND THIS POINT
IN DAYLIGHT

used to stand, and then disappear over the last crest before the front line.

The road was as lonely and deserted as of old. But magpies were still active, flying in front of me from tree to tree as in the past, and hawks seemed far more numerous. I was approaching the sugar factory at the cross roads where one turns left for Morchies, and I paused to honour the memory of a minor yet exciting escapade.

Here I had been driven by Thompson in the late evening of March 21 to learn if our pulling-out orders had reached our most forward battery in time. As Thompson drew up just beyond the sugar factory and I had got out to see how much further we could drive in safety, a Scots officer appeared revolver in hand and told me the Germans held the road in strength a couple of hundred yards ahead. I went on to see what had happened to our battery; to my astonishment – indignation too, because they had failed to let us know – I found both they and their guns had gone.

I have said I was approaching the sugar factory where one turns left for Morchies. The factory was still in ruins but a family was now living by the boilers in a house made from odds and ends. A notice stated it was ESTAMINET DE LA PAIX.

"May I have an omelette?" I asked an old woman boiling a pail of water over a fire in the ragged garden.

"Omelette?" Her voice was harsh and she shook her head. "There are no eggs."

I walked on towards Morchies, halting for a minute or two by the roadside cemetery where they had buried the men of Toc 1 killed by the premature which blew gun and detachment to bits. I was still standing there when three big farm carts came up the hill from the village. One following the other and each drawn by a pair of cantering horses, they came rattling past me like the empty limbers of a field battery on their way back to wagon lines.

In Morchies half a dozen red-brick villas were being built, but it seemed clear you had to draw your water from the pond because it no longer came in tanks by Decauville railway from Bapaume. There were still as many footpaths through the wilderness of the château garden, and the spidery crosses in the civilian cemetery still stuck out in different directions like pins in a pincushion.

I left the hamlet by the steep lane leading to Tusculum, the brigade O.P. It had been so named by reason of the relative loftiness of its situation, I imagine, and its adequacy as a viewpoint had not been questioned. But in other respects it had been a place of boredom rather than of excitement, no doubt because of its distance from the front line.

The dug-out had vanished but the wide panorama had not changed. You could no longer see the wire of the Hindenburg Line, but the ridges over which the German cavalry had come were still as bare. Standing on the bank in full view, I lit a pipe and waved my stick at Quéant. What would they have said had I done such a thing in the old days? And then I heard a dull heavy boom away to the north, up Bullecourt way. It was followed by another and another and another.

I sprang back under cover. A cloud of white smoke rose in the Agache valley. *A column of transport was marching up the Cambrai road!* My God, where was the telephone to brigade?

I pulled out my glasses, the same old glasses. The reckless cavalcade was nothing more important than the procession of farm carts from Morchies, and the smoke in the Agache valley turned out to be steam from a train. . . .

An elderly farmer in a high trap was driving towards me; he stopped and regarded me with curiosity.

"This used to be our observation post," I explained with a smile.

He nodded. "Did you hear the explosions?" he asked.

"Yes. What were they?"

"It happens every day. Always they are destroying shells." He shrugged his shoulders. "And there are plenty more to be rid of. Only last week a plough in Havrincourt touched something and an explosion followed. No one was hurt that time, but we are not always so fortunate."

He spat on the ground, wished me good night, and jogged his horse into motion.

I turned from the line. In the shallow valley before me I

saw newly turned earth, a peasant working in the field through which the Decauville light railway once had run, another peasant digging in an allotment, his spare tools resting against the massive carcase of a burnt-out tank. A faint evening mist was now advancing. Plumes of pale grey smoke were rising peacefully from the chimneys of Morchies – and I had known the whole valley filled with the smoke of bursting shells. It was growing late and I had seen enough. Soon it would be dusk, and I felt tired and very lonely.

Appendices

AGLIONBY'S ACCOUNT OF TOC 2'S SHARE
IN THE EVENTS OF MARCH 21
(See page 71)

About 5 AM I was wakened by a very heavy gas and high explosive barrage in our valley, and I got up, dressed, and put on my gas mask. Michell and Swaine came in, and I sent them to warn everyone on our side of the valley to put their masks on too. Then I went over to the B.C. Post.

It was very dark, and though I had a torch I did not know exactly where I was when I got to the road on the other side of the valley. The gas shells made so much noise that one could not hear the burst of H.E. unless it was almost on top of one. I was afraid I should get in front of No. 2 gun just as it was going to fire. I found a shelter with a light, but it was empty. Then I got on the road, but got off again as a shell burst very near and I thought I would be safer under the bank. Just after that I nearly ran into another, and then I made out the wireless mast and so found the B.C. Post.

Graham was up, and we waited for a few minutes; then Callis came in and we got two guns firing – Graham going to the left section, Callis and I to the right. We went on till dawn when the barrage ceased, though one big fellow was shelling very consistently just behind No. 6 pit and others were dropping intermittently all over the position. We all felt better when we got our masks off, mine having hurt the side of my head so much that I had to take it off every now and then to ease it.

About 8 AM I had breakfast prepared for the men and went over to the mess with Callis for some ourselves. The Boche was then shelling the light railway track beyond No. 1 pit, and now he started on the bank above; we went back to the B.C. Post and took papers and maps down the sap. All lines having been down from the start, I sent Michell to the rear

APPENDIX I

position and Timmis to brigade. The rest of the forenoon
passed without incident; we gathered from wounded officers
and men that the Boche was in our front line, and in places
in the support line. This did not sound too bad, and I sent a
runner to brigade and had lunch. I had just finished and
was lighting a cigar when Peggs, one of the servants, pointed
out a number of men on the skyline.

The battery position was in a valley running roughly east
and west, with other valleys running out of it to the north.
Just in front of the guns a valley ran off towards Vaulx, then
came the Morchies-Vaulx road, then Maricourt Wood – in
which most of the trees had been cut down but a lot of
undergrowth remained. About a thousand yards beyond the
wood the valley bends to the right, and, passing through
Lagnicourt, joins the Agache valley at Quéant. Just before
it reaches Lagnicourt a wider valley runs north towards
Noreuil. The far side of this valley, which we knew as Burton
Ridge from the O.P. on it, was the skyline from the battery
as one looks in that direction.

It was on Burton Ridge, then, that we saw large numbers
of men running about, but I could not be certain that they
were Germans. About 2 PM, being assisted by a Sapper
captain who reported that the enemy was considerably
nearer, we made up our minds that they were, and we
accordingly opened fire. They were then standing or running
about in groups; when we fired at them they moved back in
the direction of Noreuil and ceased hanging about the valley.

Then we got a written message from Callis, who shortly
after breakfast had gone to Luke O.P. about a thousand
yards on our left front, that massed Germans were coming
over our old front line. We fired at them till things in the
valley began to demand our attention more. The Boche was
now coming on in our direction from the north slope, and I
could see a wave of them had reached the wire in front of the
Morchies-Noreuil road. Accordingly I turned all guns on to
them, and when these had gone I fired at still more who had
come into the valley. I was sitting on the curved-iron roof of
the officers' mess cookhouse shouting corrections to the

B.C. Post. A machine-gun opened fire on me, and for the rest of the afternoon I sat behind the roof and looked over the top.

I was getting anxious about Callis at the O.P. because the enemy seemed to be spreading out very quickly, and while numbers of our own men were coming back through the battery I could not see any sign of fresh infantry coming up. I had already posted my surplus gunners in the defence positions round our two machine-gun posts; they had gone to their posts quickly and without confusion. I rallied such of our infantry as I had time to stop and posted them in shell holes, but they were without officers and until I could detail one of mine for the job they mostly drifted away. Much to my relief Callis turned up shortly afterwards and stayed with me by the kitchen roof. He said that the enemy were not far from the Brown Line, and that he had been driven from the O.P. by machine-gun fire.

The enemy was now up the hill and through the wire into the sunken part of the Morchies-Noreuil road. We could not stop them from getting there but we prevented them from coming any farther, and after two shells had pitched into the road the whole lot of them ran back towards Lagnicourt – a very encouraging sight. We lengthened our range and followed them over the crest, and it was some time before any came back.

In the meanwhile another force of Boche appeared in the bottom of the valley and was coming on fast. We got on to them, but they were in small parties of five or six and a good many got through into the dead ground. Their supports did not like the look of it, however, and turned back up the hill into the sunken road. About this time an enemy field gun was brought up to within fifteen hundred yards of us and started firing at us. It put one through the camouflage of No. 3 gun, and several went close above our heads. I could see the flash clearly, and I thought I could see the observer too. We fired at the cross roads at the bottom of the valley and must have hit either the gun or its ammunition, for we heard no more of it.

L

Of the enemy who came through our fire, I saw only one patrol of three men just to the left of Maricourt Wood and some five hundred yards in front of the battery. We did not use our Lewis guns on them because I made up my mind to stick to the defence scheme we had previously evolved and not disclose that we possessed machine-guns till the Boche reached the front of our battery wire. For the rest of the afternoon and while the light lasted, we went on firing at the Boche whenever we saw him.

I cannot remember the exact order in which things happened, but it was a repetition of what had gone before. I saw a big crowd of men standing on top of Burton Ridge near the O.P., and we started ranging on them. But before we got them we had to drop on to others in the neighbourhood of the sunken road, and after that we returned to the first crowd and drove them off the ridge.

About 5.30 some infantry came up from Beugny to rescue some of our men who were cut off near Lagnicourt on our right front. I told them what I knew of the situation and helped them by firing at the cross roads in the valley. This was the only infantry we saw coming up from Beugny.

It was now getting dark, and the situation was far from clear. All afternoon I had been acting on the assumption that our supports were coming up from Vaulx – this had been verified by reports from the infantry, and I had seen some of them myself. I had therefore been trying to turn the enemy northwards to get them caught, but I did not know how far south our infantry had got to or whether they were likely to hold if attacked. I had therefore already sent Graham to brigade telling him to report that I could not hold the position if attacked at night and that at the same time it would be very difficult to move the guns. We were eight hundred yards from the nearest point that could be reached by lorries or Four-Wheel Drives, and General Marshall had previously agreed that we could not move without horses.

We waited in the sap in case the Boche started his barrage once more, because I did not want to have to recross the valley in darkness. It was now very dark, and there was no shelling or machine-gun fire.

Graham returned with orders for us to stay, but this was followed by an order to move to Frémicourt. The Colonel wrote he could get no horses for us. I had already tried to borrow a team from 156 Heavy Battery, but they said that all their horses were away and not expected to return that night. Accordingly I sent word to brigade to say I could not move without horses and that I could not get any.

The men had had a long and tiring day; for the last three weeks we had been shooting night and day as well as sending big fatigue parties to make reserve positions, and no one in the battery had had two consecutive nights in bed for a month.

The Colonel sent back word that we must do our utmost to move. Accordingly I got all guns out of their pits and sent Sergeant-major Dowling to pull No. 3 gun along the light railway line – the valley had so many new shell holes and was so cut up by transport that I thought this our best chance. He got it half way, and stuck. Just then I heard that 156 Heavy Battery had got some horses, and I sent Smith to try to borrow them, which he did. Luckily the Boche was hardly firing at all. I waited till the first gun had been dragged to the road, and then went off with Callis and Graham to find the new position. We got there about 1 AM, and also found billets for the men.

The guns arrived singly, and I learned that No. 6 had fallen into a shell hole and that the combined efforts of the team of horses and of all available men could not pull it out.

We now got a little uncomfortable rest, I on someone's kitbag.

MACARTNEY'S ACCOUNT OF THE ACCIDENT
AT MIRAUMONT BRIDGE
(*See page 110*)

When dismantled for travelling, every 9·2 howitzer divides
into three parts – the Piece or barrel, Bed, and Cradle, to
give them their technical terms. These parts are loaded on
three 4-wheeled vehicles (known as transporting-carriages),
which are then coupled up one behind the other and hauled
along the roads by a 'Cat' or caterpillar tractor. The
resulting procession, if slow, is normally safe and resembles a
circus on the move. By March 22, however, Toc 1's
howitzers were no longer complete, and one or two of their
tractors and transporting-carriages had been damaged and
were now out of action.

Owing to these and other shortages two pieces were being
towed by the same tractor, and because of the length of the
barrels their respective transporters could not be coupled
together by means of the normal couplings. Thus there was
no alternative but to improvise with chains and tow-ropes –
a sad mistake as it turned out, since when on the road the
rear transporter tended to wobble about instead of following
in the tracks of the one in front of it. But there was no other
way, and it was rightly decided to carry on.

All went well till the procession reached Miraumont
Bridge, a wooden one of no great width, on the road from
Achiet-le-Petit to Miraumont. The road approached the
bridge by a sharp, almost right-angled, turn, and the lock
required to negotiate it proved too much for the chains. The
rear transporting-carriage got out of control, and after
breaking the side of the bridge it hung half suspended over
the Ancre. The bridge was already both shaky and danger-
ous, and troops retreating from Achiet-le-Petit were using it

continuously. With their help an attempt was made to pull the carriage back on the bridge, but the chains broke and it fell into the river complete with its barrel.

I was told of the accident that night, and early next morning (March 23) I went to have a look and found the carriage upside down in midstream with its wheels in the air. The muzzle of the piece was right up against the bank, which at this point was about three feet above water level. I saw from the start that it would be a gamble whether I could get it out or not. Having decided to have a try, I returned to Siege Park and brought back two Cats belonging to an 8-inch how. battery which had lost all its guns.

We soon found that the bank was too steep, and we began to make a causeway by digging it away on the slant. We dug all day, and in the evening we hitched on the two Cats and pulled. The piece moved only a few inches. Throughout the afternoon we had been intermittently shelled by a big H.V. gun which may or may not have been shooting at the adjoining railway embankment.

The plan I worked out that night entailed the use of a gin or three-legged crane – with it I thought I could lift the whole carriage clear of the bank and with the further help of a Cat turn it right side up on its wheels. At dawn on the 24th, therefore, I set off in a lorry in search of Ordnance Workshops, which I heard had moved to Mailly-Maillet. I went there, only to be told they had moved on to Sailly, a village north of Courcelles. I found them there and asked them for a gin, but through the confusion of the retreat they could not find one. It was now about noon, and I decided the best thing was to go back to Miraumont Bridge and render the piece useless. I drove there with much difficulty, meeting very heavy traffic all the way. A party of Royal Engineers was now working on the causeway and trying to improve its surface by means of sleepers from the railway line, but it was no use. After trying in vain to remove the breech block from the barrel I took off the wheels, brakes, and winding chains of the carriage, and returned to Siege Park for the night.

Next morning (25th) I got hold of a couple of gunners and

A.S.C. men and went back to the bridge to have another try at removing the breech block, but we were stymied through lack of the proper tools. While making our final effort we heard that the Germans were in Achiet-le-Petit, and by now our infantry was in full retreat. On seeing some of them come over the near crest in open order and post a machine-gunner a couple of hundred yards away from us I decided it was high time we cleared off.

FROM THE OTHER SIDE OF THE HILL

Additional light is thrown on the March Retreat by the following:

FROM ENEMY SOURCES

Extracts from an unposted letter, written at Puisieux early in April by a Sergeant-major of the 46th Infantry Regiment:

We had great confidence in our artillery. The guns, which included German, Austrian, and captured guns from Russia, stood almost on top of one another. The Quéant-Pronville area was full of batteries which had been put in position some days before. The crews for many of these arrived only on the night of the 20th.

At 5.0 AM the bombardment started, gas being fired on the enemy artillery. At 9.0 AM there was a pause in the firing so that the Tommies should come out of their positions: ten minutes later it commenced again on their trenches, and at ten o'clock we attacked. At 10.15 we were already in their trenches, and the 58th Regiment in the enemy second line. The few Scotsmen remaining alive were taken prisoners and sent to the rear, their cigarettes being first taken from them. We had by this time several casualties. In the evening we were in possession of Doignies, where we captured several guns. . . .

Owing to the rain the roads are half a metre deep in mud. The horses are dying like flies; I counted 37 on a stretch of road four kilometres long, the majority having been killed by artillery fire.

A prisoner of the same Regiment, captured near Bucquoy on April 5 stated:

On the 21st British heavy artillery obtained a direct hit on the Regimental Battle Headquarters of the 58th Infantry

Regiment near Boursies, killing five officers including the Regimental Commander and several men.

Notes on a lecture delivered on March 18 and taken from the diary of an officer of the 119th Grenadier Regiment:

The direction of the main attack is due west towards the coast, Abbeville, and Boulogne, with the intention of separating the English from the French: the blow to be delivered chiefly against the former. The plans are so thorough that failure is impossible: if the attack fails in one place it is to be broken off and another place tried.

Extracts from the diary of a dead officer of the 73rd Fusilier Regiment:

20.4.18. We had indented for a car the day before from Group, and so we set out in the direction of Mory. The run through the country recently regained was interesting. Quéant, for a start, left a disconsolate impression although everything had already been neatly tidied up and the Tommies were already working hard on improving the roads. The sight of the prisoners was rather depressing. War weary and dejected, no more of that supercilious, haughty bearing as last year after the battle of the Somme. . . . Thus war has changed a smiling countryside into a desert, and the only explanation I can find for the obstinacy of our enemies is that they believe all is lost.

In the hottest hours of the day I walked to Bapaume, where the afternoon train leaves for Cambrai. What a sight the town is! A few gables were still standing, but otherwise there was nothing of a single house left. Tommy's camps outside the town look like negro villages in Central Africa. From Bapaume our road took us along the erstwhile English Lines of Communication. Tommy had laid out plenty of railroads for us, and the rolling stock we captured renders us valuable service. Along the railway English ammunition was still lying in heaps. He had to leave all sorts of things behind. Prisoners were lending a hand to keep the track in repair.

APPENDIX 3

FROM BRITISH SOURCES
Information from an escaped prisoner of the 51st (Highland) Division:

At the commencement of the enemy offensive on March 21, this private soldier was in a dug-out near the Bapaume-Cambrai road at Louverval. Gas was mixed with the first barrage and the British garrison kept underground. The enemy got round the left flank and rear of the position in great force, marching in artillery formation with complete companies, and overwhelmed all resistance. Very large numbers of German wounded were distributed all over the area north of Louverval, and British prisoners were employed carrying them to dressing stations. The German wounded were very callously treated, and bandages and dressings ran out. Between 10 AM and noon field batteries were being brought into action north of Louverval near our old front line. Prisoners of war were taken to Denain via Cambrai, the hospitals on the way being packed. The traffic consisted entirely of horse-transport in poor condition drawn by Russian ponies and ill-fed horses. The roads were crowded but not blocked, and there were large numbers of walking wounded to be seen.

A Prisoner-of-War Company was formed and employed on repairing the roads round Lagnicourt. This escaped private soldier acquired a German greatcoat: some days later he hid in a cellar in Lagnicourt. Having found a German cap, gas-mask, and trousers, he made his way via Vaulx and Frémicourt to Bapaume. Hutments and villages were all occupied, but both by day and by night the roads were nearly free from transport. The old C.C.S. at Grévillers was still used as such. He got past a control-post outside Bapaume by getting on to a tractor-drawn heavy gun and letting the driver do the talking, and passed all who accosted him by paying no attention.

After a night in Bapaume he proceeded via the railway into our lines near Puisieux.

APPENDIX 4

There may be readers who would like to know something of the later history of a few of those who have appeared in this book, and if in writing about them my own life-thread at times becomes entwined with theirs I ask to be excused, since all were my friends.

Shortly after Armistice Day the Colonel received a C.M.G.[1] and a D.S.O. in the same Gazette. He was pleased and I think surprised; he was also remorseful for having done so little for his battery commanders in that way. But it was now too late. Soon afterwards, having astonished us all by marrying – the officers of the Brigade subscribed and as a wedding present gave him the brigade crest modelled in silver – he retired from the army. On his honeymoon he visited Mexico, where as the result of a revolution his wife's family estates had been sequestrated – salvage again! En route they travelled through the United States to El Paso to consult a real estate agent about conducting negotiations across the frontier; on the strength of only a few days' acquaintance the agent offered him a partnership, saying that though a Britisher he was the first honest man he had yet met. The Colonel, much touched, refused; he explained he had fully earned his army pension by years of hard work abroad and now he wished to live at home to enjoy it. Amazed that such a good offer could have been turned down, the Texan found it hard to take the Colonel's No for a final answer.

On their return from Mexico the Colonel and his wife spent the best part of a year motoring throughout the length

[1] At that period the Companionship of the Order of St. Michael and St. George was awarded to many successful Lieutenant-Colonels; later it became reserved for members of the Colonial and Foreign Services.

and breadth of England looking for a house. They inspected about eighty advertised for sale in *Country Life* and similar papers, discovered each one had a snag of some kind or another, and ended up by buying a villa on the outskirts of Woking – I remember its front windows had borders of stained glass, its front door too.

When I was married in 1925 the Colonel sent a wedding present of four silver napkin rings engraved Toc 1, Toc 2, Toc 3, and Toc 4 respectively; he wrote that Toc 1 was for me, Toc 2 for my wife, Toc 3 and Toc 4 were to be reserved for our first two children, and any in excess of that number would have to be provided with napkin rings by ourselves.

By now, as these things do, the Brigade's annual reunion dinner in London had lapsed, and I next saw the Colonel when he invited my wife and me to stay overnight with them in Woking. On arrival I was taken on a thorough tour of inspection. He had fitted out part of the garage as a work-shop, and on its shelves I saw a formidable array of tins, all neatly painted in variegated colours. According to the paint code-card hanging on the wall, each contained a different size or kind of nail, nut, bolt, or screw.

At six o'clock the following morning he knocked on our bedroom door and gruffly ordered me to get up and dress and join him downstairs. He was waiting in gumboots and his old British warm, and after a cup of strong tea – to remind us of Ypres and elsewhere, he said – we went first to the garage. There he handed me a spade. He took one too, and I followed him to the bottom of the garden, where a narrow stream divided his land from his neighbour's. It was almost dry, and we stood a few yards apart and shovelled earth from the far bank to his – by doing a little every fine day, he explained, he had already increased the area of his property by over a hundred square yards. We dug for an hour in silence and unobserved. My wife and I had a long way to motor, and I was unable to go on digging with him after breakfast. At Christmas time some six months later he wrote that the stream, swollen by winter rains, had reverted to its original course and that all his work had been wasted.

I cannot recall that I saw him again. For a few years we corresponded at increasing intervals, and then we lost touch with one another. I am very sorry I did not make the opportunity of calling in to see him during the 1939-45 war, when on occasions I had to go from the north to the War Office. I do not know, nor can I even guess, what he would have said had I arrived in uniform, for by that time I had become a Colonel. Very properly, I think, he would have ignored it altogether, and he would have talked to me as if I had still been his Adjutant. I know I would have preferred it that way. He was still living in Woking when he died in 1955 at the age of 86. He had certainly lived to enjoy his pension.

Pargiter left Toc 1 for hospital treatment – his old N.W. Frontier wound was giving trouble again. Then he served with the British Military Mission to Lithuania, came back to England to go to the Staff College, and returned to India for a second tour of duty. There he commanded a Mountain Battery and became a Staff College instructor at Quetta. Home once more, he went to the Imperial Defence College and did two spells at the War Office. During his time there he had to anticipate the disastrous consequences of the political decision to hand over the Irish ports to the Government of Eire; he also had to deal with the problems of the defence of Singapore. Of less moment, we sometimes fished together on the borders of Westmorland and Yorkshire, and the day he lost his landing-net in the Lune I took a cine picture which still shows only too clearly how, unseen by both of us, it slipped in off the rock beside him. Shortly before the war we visited his wife and him at Blackdown, and together we all saw the last of the Aldershot Tattoos. On the outbreak of war he went off to France in command of the 1st Anti-Aircraft Brigade.

Promoted Major-General in 1940, he was posted to command 4th Anti-Aircraft Division at Chester; I happened to be one of his Regimental Commanders. For a hectic week or two at the time of Dunkirk he was recalled to the War Office; next he was sent to Newcastle upon Tyne to command 7th

Anti-Aircraft Division – to which a few months later I was posted as G.S.O.1. On hearing I was coming to him he wrote to say he would much have preferred a G.1 with Staff College qualifications, but since he understood none were available he would as soon have me as anyone else. Furthermore, he wrote, he did not wish me or anybody else to think that he had applied for me. Once I found my feet – no easy mental or gymnastic task for an untrained Territorial Lieutenant-Colonel – I think I served him as well as could be expected. At any rate I had a number of happy months with him; he was as successful and revered a Divisional Commander as he had been a battery commander. At typically short notice he was transferred to an A.A. Division in the south of England, and finally he was sent to Algiers where as M.G.A.A. (Major-General Anti-Aircraft) of the Western Mediterranean he took command of all anti-aircraft forces in North Africa and Italy, British and American alike, till the end of the war. He then retired, and later became a Colonel-Commandant of the Royal Artillery.

He lives in Devonshire, he still fishes, and he has taught himself Braille. Since his retirement he has turned 40 printed books into 247 Braille volumes, all for students' libraries and mostly history. 'So my retiring days have not been entirely wasted,' he writes, and continues, 'My prevailing feeling, when I look back, is how much better I could have done things, and how many mistakes and unkindnesses I could have avoided, if only I had known then as much as I do now. But I suppose that is common to all the aged. If youth but knew. . . .'

After three years at Cambridge Walker worked for a time in his brother's firm on the Baltic, selling parcels and cargoes of Australian wheat. But he had set his heart on school-mastering, and an illness with two winters abroad gave him the chance to think again. He then wrote to his ex-head-master, Alington, and was promptly invited to teach at Eton for a term, during which he lived with the Alington family in 'Cloisters.' The following term he went to teach at Winchester, and there he has remained. As senior history master for twenty-five years he was behind the expansion which has made Winchester historians no less numerous or respectable than Winchester classics, and as befits a Salopian he modernized Boat Club, was the first to put Winchester into eights, and took them to Henley. He was an admirable housemaster, and Toc 5 – for my wife and I did have one more child than the Colonel's napkin rings permitted – went to his house.

Though now officially retired, he continues to coach boats and history scholars; he lives in the old wharf house beside the Itchen, whereon and not for nothing he is still known as the Admiral. I forget how many of his house and history men have already been to visit him in his retirement; the number even now runs into hundreds. Each year he comes north to see us, and I keep pressing him to write a book himself.

I did not again meet Gardiner until a few years ago, when as an Inspector of the Ministry of Health he came to Chester to conduct a ministerial inquiry into the allocation of the waters of the River Dee. I asked him home to dinner; before he accepted he asked if I had any interest, vested or otherwise, in the subject of his inquiry. I assured him that except as an unwilling drinker of its water I had none, and he came. He was not quite the Gardiner of thirty-five years earlier – he had become more judicial and much tidier. But he was every bit as delightful, and he dismissed the protracted proceedings at Chester – since they were fully reported in the press I am guilty of no breach of confidence – by saying, "God has put a limit on the amount of water in the Dee, but unfortunately none on the number of people wanting to take some out of it."

In the summer of 1959 he was awarded a C.B.E. – he had become the Ministry's Deputy Chief Engineer. A few weeks later, just before his intended retirement, he died suddenly while at work.

Fulton recently moved from Merseyside to North Wales,

and I am sorry to say he is not as well as he might be. He has just retired from the firm which he has served, mainly as a travelling salesman, since the end of the 1914-18 war – much to its grief, also to the grief of many of his customers. His five daughters are all married, and he has so many grandchildren that he has lost count of the exact number. During his retirement he intends to raise and tend a flock of geese; I have asked him if they appeal to him because they remind him of 90th Brigade, and for once he had no ready answer.

There is a subaltern I dare not name; he supped with us recently when on Assize in Liverpool. He is a High Court Judge, and in presence – and in weight – he is very different from the shy and slender youngster of Toc 5 who, pale and tense of face, on more occasions than one gave me a deferential salute and handed me a long-overdue return which, Sir, the Major says to tell you he fears may be rather late.

As for myself, I left the railway in the early 'twenties to join the family firm, and apart from some years away during the 1939-45 war I have been there ever since. I have written a book or two and helped to found a Residential Adult College, but I cannot think I have done much else.

The telephone drill which the Colonel so forcefully expounded has remained part of me throughout my life. I have as great a horror of the word 'Hullo' as he ever had, and to this day I rarely ask our switchboard girls at the office to get me a person or a number without holding on for him or it myself. "Shake the microphone and speak into it properly," I can still hear him saying irritably. . . .

In my pipe dreams I sometimes wonder, had he been serving in the army twenty years later, how he would have dealt with any women under his command. I think it likely he would have reduced many a radar plotter to tears. On the other hand as many would have loved him, because on those occasions when anyone pleased him he could be almost benign. Yet, however bad or good they were at their jobs,

I do not think he would ever have been conscious of their sex.

Telephone drill and accuracy in details was but a small part of what the Colonel taught me. The army was my University, he my Tutor, and I conclude by quoting three lines from a letter he wrote to me from Belgium in January 1919:

'I don't know that I taught you much in our time together, but I think you learnt that if a job's worth doing it's worth doing as well as you possibly can, which is about all the secret of success anyway.'